# Praise for *BIFF*™ *for CoParent Communication*

"*Functional Communication between coparents in shared parenting arrangements is essential to share child-focused information, to coordinate children's schedules, education and health needs and to manage and resolve issues that arise. These three experienced authors provide an incredibly practical resource for parents who struggle to establish and maintain BIFF communication. The guidance in this book is also invaluable to mental health and legal professionals who work with high-conflict coparents. What a great contribution to children's healthy development!*"

— MATTHEW J. SULLIVAN, Ph.D, co-author of
*Overcoming the Alienation Crisis: 33 Coparenting Solutions*

"*Coparenting is hard in any circumstance and when doing it with someone that has a high conflict personality, can seem impossible. The first step is to admit that you are outmatched in every way except for the ability to learn new skills related to the high conflict personality. My life did not change until I began to read and understand and start using tools like BIFF. I couldn't help my children because I couldn't help myself and until I learned new tools, felt hopeless. Using BIFF will give you hope that change is possible.*"

— AL C., coparent

"*Eddy, Burns and Chafin welcome you to the dojo of BIFF. In this book, these three masters of the martial arts of coparenting discord teach us how to sidestep every attack, always keenly focused on the child's well-being. Let the blamespeakers taunt and provoke and bait as they may. Let the damning emails and text messages and social media provocateurs do their worst. Armed with this valuable volume's simple, clear and common sense skills, you will defuse conflict, improve communication, facilitate consistency, minimize unnecessary litigation, and raise healthier kids. Thank you, Sensei, for sharing these vital lessons in healthy co-parenting. Invaluable.*"

— BENJAMIN D. GARBER, Ph.D, author of
*Holding Tight/Letting Go; Mending Fences*; and
*The Healthy Parenting Series*

"*Judges often issue court orders that require coparents to communicate only in writing as a way to eliminate or reduce the conflict between them. In fact, written communications can be just as damaging as verbal ones. Judges' orders would be more effective if they recommended this book to high conflict parents and urged them to use the BIFF skills and techniques in every written communication between them.*"

— KAREN S. ADAM
*Retired Family Court Judge*

*"As a coparent deep in a dysfunctional, high-conflict coparenting relationship, I appreciate the insight in this book tremendously. My only regret is that I haven't read it sooner! Now, with the skills and tools I've gained from this read, I'm better prepared to respond with respect for myself and my coparent while standing firm and hopefully guiding us together to a better, healthier way to communicate with each other. Thank you, BIFF!"*

— BIANCA S., coparent

*"BIFF is a skeleton key for unlocking the gridlock of high conflict coparenting. Readers will learn a simple but powerful solution for a host of divorce and separation problems. Parents who develop BIFF skills will save themselves and their children a lot of emotional upset. Highly recommended."*

— JOHN A. MORAN, Ph.D, co-author of
   *Overcoming the Alienation Crisis:*
   *33 Coparenting Solutions*

# BIFF™

## for CoParent Communication

Your Guide to Difficult Texts,
Emails, and Social Media Posts

Bill Eddy, LCSW, Esq.
Annette Burns, JD
Kevin Chafin, LPC

UNHOOKED BOOKS
an imprint of High Conflict Institute Press
Scottsdale, Arizona

Copyright © 2020 by Bill Eddy, Annette Burns, Kevin Chafin
Unhooked Books, an imprint of High Conflict Institute Press
7701 E. Indian School Rd., Ste. F
Scottsdale, AZ 85251
www.unhookedbooks.com

Cover design by Julian León, The Missive

ISBN: 978-1950057108
eISBN: 978-1950057177

Library of Congress Control Number: 2020945936

**Also by Bill Eddy**

**Also by Annette Burns**

# DEDICATION

*I dedicate this book to the many separated and divorcing parents
who have shared their stories, their struggles, and successes with
me over the past forty years. They get much of the credit
for helping me develop the BIFF method of coparent
communication. This is for you!*

— **Bill**

*My part in this book is dedicated to the Association of Family and
Conciliation Courts (AFCC), without which my contributions
simply wouldn't have been possible. AFCC's dedication to
families embroiled in family court and the professionals that
serve them cannot be overstated.*

— **Annette**

*Somewhere off in the future, the children of my clients will grow
into adults. They hold us accountable for improving their lives.
I dedicate this book to them.*

— **Kevin**

# CONTENTS

## SECTION 1

## SECTION 2

# How BIFF Was Born

BIFF was born in March 2007 in Phoenix, Arizona, when I was giving a workshop about managing high conflict divorce cases in family courts. It was the first in a series of trainings that I was doing with Megan Hunter around the United States, the year before we founded High Conflict Institute. There were about 20 lawyers, mediators, therapists, and two judges in attendance that day.

One of the techniques I taught them was using an EAR Statement®, which is a calm way of responding in person to someone who was upset or angry. I had developed this method a few years earlier when I discovered that my counseling background could help in calming my clients as a lawyer and in mediation sessions. It made it easy to remember to make statements showing Empathy, Attention and Respect. Since law and mediation clients were often upset and sometimes verbally attacked me, I found that this was an easy way to remember what to do when I was under stress. As I was giving the training, the class said this was a really useful technique because it was so easy to remember, because they were often under stress too.

Then, at some point in the middle of the training, one of the judges asked me "What can we do about these awful emails that some of the parents are sending to each other and then filing with the court? Each one is pointing the finger at the other one, saying how outrageously the other is behaving. Yet it seems like both of them are acting badly, sometimes equally badly, but they just can't see it."

By then, I had been a therapist for a dozen years, followed by 14 years as a family lawyer and mediator. I had had many of those cases with nasty emails and I had been teaching my clients to avoid engaging in them—choosing their battles as to when to respond and when to just ignore them. I hadn't really thought much about how I was telling them to write those emails, but when the judge asked the question it got me thinking about what worked and what didn't work. After all, I had a few hundred cases by then and had seen (and been part of writing) probably a thousand emails and letters in divorce cases.

"Certainly, they need to be brief," I said to the judges and the rest of the group. "From my experience, the longer the email the more trouble one gets into. From what I've seen, a paragraph is usually sufficient, even in response to a several page email or letter."

"I also think they need to be informative," I added to the class. "Just straight information. No opinions, no emotions, no defensiveness because that's what escalates things. And that's not easy to do, but I have been coaching my clients on writing that way and they actually feel better doing that. This way they can save time and emotional energy by avoiding all the venting—even when the other person is mostly venting."

"Lastly," I said. "I think they need to be friendly. Just friendly enough to calm the conversation. It could be a nice greeting—like 'Thanks for responding'—or a pleasant closing, like 'Have a good weekend.' I try to tell my clients to think of how they would write to a friend. This keeps them from making things worse from their end."

One of the judges was busy writing this down and looked up and said: "That's BIF! B-I-F!"

"Hm," I replied. "I never thought of it that way before."

"Then you need another 'F,' and you have BIFF," the other judge said. "Easy to remember, just like EAR."

I immediately thought that the next most important thing about emails and letters was that they should end the hostile conversation instead of escalating it.

"Then the other 'F' would be Firm," I said. "You want them to end the hostilities without putting out a hook to get the other person to respond. (No more: 'What do you think of that, Buddy?' at the end of an email.) And that can be really hard to do, but so important. So, BIFF would be Brief, Informative, Friendly, and Firm. Thanks! That makes it easier to remember."

Everyone was pleased to have it be so simple and it was one of the great take-aways from the training—for me as well as the participants. Yet I also realized that it wasn't simple at all and that I sometimes spent half an hour or more helping a client feel confident that their email response wasn't showing weakness because it didn't include any hostile remarks like the email they were responding to. But I also realized that BIFF sounds strong.

Later that year I wrote an article about it called "Responding to Hostile Mail (B.I.F.F.)." But at some point

I realized that we needed to say more than just "BIFF." It might have been after a I had a conversation with a man from Australia at a training I gave in Toronto later in 2007.

The Toronto training included family lawyers, therapists and mediators, and I told them about BIFF for emails and letters. Afterward, at the end of the all-day training, a man came up to me and said that he was from Australia and that BIFF already had a common usage there. "In Australia, a BIFF means a 'faht.' You might want to think of a different word for Australia."

To be honest, I wasn't sure (with his accent and my hearing) whether he had said "fart" or "fight." I was tired, so I simply thanked him and told myself I would need to look it up. I liked BIFF and didn't want to change it. But in 2008 I would be giving my first trainings in Australia, so I knew I needed to understand if there was really a problem.

When I arrived in Melbourne, Australia, I was riding a bus a day or so before giving my first training and a headline jumped out at me from a newspaper another rider was reading. It said something like "Fans Want More BIFF at Games." That clinched it: BIFF was a fight between players, with them trying to punch each other. Whew, I was relieved to find out in advance that a BIFF wasn't a fart!

But did that eliminate my use of the word BIFF for this communication technique? It occurred to me that our BIFFs were really *responses* to verbal punches from people in a high conflict divorce or workplace dispute or other setting. In Australia, I would emphasize that the technique was a BIFF *Response*, and thus BIFF Response® was born. Years later Megan and I trademarked the term—in the United States *and* Australia!

# Preface

In 2011, I wrote a full book about the method, with about twenty examples (*BIFF: Quick Responses to High Conflict People, Their Personal Attacks, Hostile Email and Social Media Meltdowns*). Then, in 2014, I added a new method for a second edition: Coaching for BIFF Responses, which became a new chapter in the book, one that could be used by counselors, coaches and even family members to help each other. But the interest in this method has grown exponentially, especially in the area of coparenting after a separation or divorce. Time for a BIFF book exclusively devoted to coparenting communication.

— Bill Eddy, September 2020

# About This Book

This book is written by the three of us. Annette (a family lawyer) and Kevin (a family therapist) have been using and teaching BIFF communications with coparents for years, almost from the birth of BIFF. With their added expertise and examples, this book addresses numerous coparenting issues and how you can use BIFF communications for calmer discussions and decision-making.

This book teaches you how you can use BIFF communications for starting conversations, as well as for responding to hostile or misinformed emails, texts, and so forth. That's why this book is about *BIFF communications*, not just *BIFF responses*. This book stands on its own, or you can also get the original BIFF book (2nd Edition, as described above), for its broader application including non-parenting situations and explanations of high conflict personalities.

We have used the same general format throughout much of the book: Giving an example of someone's hostile or misinformed communication, followed by a negative (but tempting) response, followed by a positive BIFF example. The BIFF communications are explained so that the reader can become more and more familiar with the nuances of writing BIFFs in their own new situations. Some examples we use are drawn from real situations but well-disguised while others are totally made up.

We have tried to cover some of the most common areas of coparent communication and potential conflict. By the end of the book you will have this simple method clear in your mind and should be ready for almost any situation. Of course, we encourage you to get feedback on your BIFF communications before you send them out, just to check for hidden problems you may have missed while reading your own writing (we all have this problem sometimes). On the other hand, there often isn't time to get such feedback, so that we encourage you to ask yourself the coaching questions as described in the book before you hit Send.

We also recognize that we have written this during the COVID-19 pandemic and that new and more tense situations have arisen for coparents that none of us anticipated. So please use the principles we have explained in this book to help you deal with any situations that we did not address here and perhaps no one has ever faced before. Just know that you are not alone in facing many of these problems, and that you may be able to help yourself and your children by calming a conflict using BIFF.

The structure of the book is this:

**Section 1** explains the basics of a BIFF communication, including what not to write (Blamespeak), how to write a BIFF, and some nuances (avoiding the three A's).

**Section 2** includes about thirty examples of BIFF communications in many common and important areas, including educational decisions, healthcare, activities and so on. Annette and Kevin get the credit here for the examples and most of the analysis of the examples.

**Section 3** addresses the key issues of how to coach someone else for giving a BIFF communication and that, ultimately, it is up to you to influence how your coparent responds by how you communicate with him or her.

The Appendix includes three articles addressing some standards regarding coparent boundaries, what to tell the children about a high conflict coparent (including what not to say), and a brief explanation of an EAR Statement,® which is designed for in-person conversations in contrast to BIFF responses which are designed for written communication.

## Writing Us

Lastly, one of the most exciting things for all of us is getting feedback from parents about how writing BIFF communications has calmed the writing of both coparents, even when the other one doesn't know the method! It's contagious in a good way. We hope you find this helpful and will let us know how it works for you.

If you want to send us an example of a BIFF that you are particularly proud of, please send it with the full written conversation of both parents so we can see how you resisted the urge to escalate and instead calmed the conflict. You can send correspondence to us at info@highconflictinstitute.com.

You can learn more about BIFF and practice BIFF at ConflictPlaybook.com.

We wish you all the best!

> — Bill Eddy, Annette Burns and Kevin Chafin
> September 2020

# CHAPTER ONE

# Blamespeak

You are holding in your hands the key to peaceful coparent communication. Since 2007, we have taught approximately half a million people the BIFF communication method through our books and seminars. The feedback has been overwhelmingly positive. So many people tell us that they have shared this method with others, so there may be about a million people using this method today. You are in good company. The more people that use this method, the more peaceful the world will be.

We are very excited and pleased that you have chosen to learn the BIFF method of coparent communication. We believe it will make your life easier and less stressed, even when being attacked, accused, or misinformed in writing by a coparent—or anyone! BIFF communications are simple but take practice. By the time you are done reading this book and its examples, you may be able to write BIFF communications in your sleep!

## It's NOT All Your Fault!

You know that coparenting is a unique and fascinating and often frustrating relationship. Even when parents are still a couple, it can be fraught with hurt and blame. But between separated parents, it can become a minefield for fear, anger, and bullying. Trying to coparent with someone who is hurt and vengeful can result in communications that don't benefit and in fact hurt your child.

Hearing things like "This is all YOUR fault" or "You're a disgrace and a terrible parent" have long-lasting detrimental effects. They make you, a parent, feel worthless and less than adequate. Even if someone thinks they can handle verbal abuse, long-term damage is done to a relationship if verbal communications aren't improved. Fortunately, there are things you can do on your own that will help your communications with a coparent who may be (putting it mildly) a very poor communicator. However, the BIFF method of communicating will help you with any coparent, including a reasonable one. BIFF helps you stay reasonable most of the time regardless of how your coparent communicates.

Learning not to take things personally is perhaps the best skill you can develop as a coparent. Problems that arise are not (necessarily) about you, no matter what you are accused of. If you know you're doing your best in a given situation, then you can be more confident that accusations made against you *are not about you!*

Most of us have said something accusatory or mean when we've *lost it* with our coparent. We can work to make sure those attacks don't happen too often. Some people communicate in bullying or angry ways often, or exclusively. The first and best way to deal with those angry communicators are to know that the personal attacks are not about you. They are about the *blamer's* inability to communicate, to control himself, and to solve problems.

When people repeatedly use personal attacks, try to think of them as ineffective communicators, and of yourself as the antidote to their communications. Remember that someone who is constantly blaming and bullying lacks skills for dealing well with conflict. They are unable to share responsibility for problems or for solving them. The way they communicate and handle themselves *increases* conflict by making every issue intensely personal and by taking no responsibility for anything.

Some people are preoccupied with blaming others and likely believe that everyone else in the world is responsible for their problems. The people they blame are their *targets of blame*, and when it comes to parenting, you, the coparent, are the target. They speak what we often call Blamespeak: Attack, defend—and attack again. We wrote this book to help you, the coparent, respond to your coparent and others who try to trigger you with hostile emails, texts, social media postings, rumors or just plain difficult behavior.

We also want to help you write useful and substantive communications about your children that will reduce the conflict your children are exposed to. Before we explain how to write BIFF communications and responses, we'll give you a brief understanding of how Blamespeak works so that you can successfully shift a conversation to be less angry and even productive. Once you know what *not to do*, as well as what to do, you can improve the communication process with them, even without their help. Your BIFF communications will be better if you understand this and work on this skill.

## Patterns of Blamespeak

Those who use a lot of Blamespeak have a repeated pattern of aggressive behavior that increases conflict rather than reducing or resolving it. It may be part of their personalities—how they automatically and unconsciously think, feel and behave—and they carry this pattern with them in most relationships, not just the relationship with the coparent. Or, they may use Blamespeak in a difficult moment when their emotions take over and they lose control of how to speak appropriately, but then catch themselves and become more reasonable again. This book is designed to help you respond or initiate communications regardless of the other person's behavior.

When people have a repeated pattern of using Blamespeak, we think of them as *high conflict people* (HCPs). Such people have a pattern of repeated behavior that includes the following four primary characteristics:

1. **Preoccupation with blaming others**
   (people close to them or people in authority)
2. **All-or-nothing thinking**
   (one person is all good, another is all bad)
3. **Unmanaged emotions**
   (exaggerated anger, fear, sadness—out of proportion to events)
4. **Extreme behavior**
   (yelling, hitting, lying, spreading rumors, impulsive actions, etc.)

If you recognize this pattern in your coparent, DO NOT TELL THEM YOU THINK THAT! It will add significantly to their defensiveness for days or months or years. Just use your awareness to remember to adapt how you deal with him or her, and to remember even more strongly to use BIFF responses as much as possible.

However, our focus in this book will be on how to respond to Blamespeak rather than trying to analyze the other person's personality. Just be prepared for some people to be stuck in Blamespeak while others may be able to more easily stop themselves after receiving your BIFF communication. Throughout the book we will mention some of the common predictable behavior of HCPs and how you can respond to it with BIFF communications.

Blamespeak seems to have increased rapidly during our lifetimes, although it's likely been around forever. Everyone loses their temper and control at times and uses a form of Blamespeak occasionally (hopefully rarely), but separated coparents may use it a lot.

Blamespeak often sounds childish and immature, although the person using it isn't likely to recognize that. It's similar to the disrespectful way that young children talk to their siblings or their parents in anger before they mature and learn self-restraint: "I hate you!" "You're an idiot!" "I'm never speaking to you again!"

Society and the media in general promote a level of this, including reality TV and news shows that encourage speakers to interrupt, yell, and insult each other—to gain viewers and sell products. Unlike children, who may have these outbursts and then go on playing nicely together, adults engaged in Blamespeak usually don't play nicely afterwards. Blamespeak is a way of getting attention at a time of rapid change, a way of being heard and not ignored, often by people who have a great fear of being ignored or marginalized.

In the coparenting relationship, one parent may feel marginalized by court orders that limit time, or by the failure of the parents' relationship. A parent may feel that his or her feelings and opinions don't count unless they are expressed in a forceful and blaming way. The media has taught us that if someone wants attention, he or she needs to forcefully take it. Blamespeak is a cheap and easy way to grab attention in our society. Our brains are wired to pay the most attention to emergencies. Being aggressive and exaggerating situations and blame does tend to grab attention because it *feels* like there is an emergency.

Unfortunately, electronic media in particular has the ability to manipulate emergency responses in our brain wiring, especially when the same blaming words and angry tone are repeated, over and over and over again. The repetition and appearance in electronic media give the blaming words exaggerated power, which hijacks our attention and makes us believe we *are* in danger and *should be* more anxious than circumstances warrant. It's difficult to ignore loud, dramatic and intense Blamespeak, both in the news and on your own computer screen.

### Recognizing Blamespeak

You can recognize Blamespeak by the following characteristics:

# Blamespeak

1. It's usually **emotionally intense** and out of proportion to the issues. If your coparent is furious and raging about a 10-minute change in a parenting time schedule, it's probably Blamespeak. Sometimes Blamespeak is calm, but it can be subtle and passive aggressive and bring out the worst in a reasonable person's response. Blamespeak is rarely boring.

2. It's **very personal**: Blamespeak insults your intelligence, sanity, memory, ethics, choices, sex life, looks, or morals. For example, your coparent might claim that you are exposing your child to multiple affairs, or that you are addicted to drugs, or that you have lost your mind, even when there is absolutely no basis for these claims.

3. **It's all your fault**: the Blamespeaker feels no responsibility for the problem or the solution. He or she may say that you have to fix a problem that they really created, but they can't see their part in it at all.

4. **It's out of context**: Blamespeak ignores anything good you've done and ignores all of the bad the Blamespeaker has done. Your coparent might begin a statement saying: "You never" or "You always" in regard to your child, when in fact you were only late once or missed one meeting, or did take the child to the doctor several times that the other parent simply can't remember.

5. It's often **shared with others** to emphasize how blame-*worthy* you are and how blame*less* the speaker is. Some Blamespeakers have no sense of shame, embarrassment, or boundaries. He or she may speak negatively about you in public. Unfortunately, Blamespeak often sounds

believable to those who aren't informed about your situation or who don't know the Blamespeaker well enough to know how out of proportion the statements are.

6. You have an **intensely negative gut feeling** about the Blamespeak. This gut feeling might sicken you, make you feel fearful, guilty, helpless, and/or very angry. You may even feel you have to blame someone else and go looking for your own target of blame.

7. You find yourself compelled to respond with Blamespeak of your own. It is extremely hard to step back to prepare a reasonable response, or to decide not to respond at all. You feel you can't allow the outrageous, accusing statements about you to go unanswered, and you feel you must respond immediately! Instead, you can analyze the situation and decide whether a response is appropriate or not. And if you respond, make sure it's a BIFF.

## Responding to Blamespeak

Many people initially react to Blamespeak with Blamespeak of their own (you might call this "counter Blamespeak"). This happens to almost everyone before you learn about BIFF communications. These counter attacks are a normal human response to the unrestrained aggressive behavior of others. Your counter attack might even be true. But remember, pointing out the Blamespeaker's bad behavior or errors won't change anything and will usually just escalate the situation. For example, you might be tempted to say or write:

"YOU'RE the one who's stupid, crazy and unethical! You lied to our son about why he had a babysitter last week."

"Look in the mirror, Buddy! Here's what you'll see..."

"You're an idiot if you think I'm going to respond to your long-winded B.S. and incoherent babbling and lies!"

"Remember it was just last month when YOU forgot to pay his lunch bill!"

"If you don't do something about this, I'm going to tell everyone that you're a tax cheater and you let our child see porn on your computer."

"You have no clue what you are talking about and should just shut up! You never even attended the court-ordered parenting class!"

This counter Blamespeak not only doesn't work but also makes you look like a possible high conflict person to those outside the situation. The Blamespeaker will use your reaction to justify a new round of Blamespeak, and the back and forth will go on and on, with no resolution or good result for your children. The key is to not over-react, and instead to recognize and manage your emotions. Then respond relatively quickly but not impulsively, with a BIFF response to the Blamespeak. Or, as we'll discuss, the key may be to not respond at all. In some situations, this is the best idea. But in many other situations a BIFF is better.

# Conclusion

In this first chapter, we wanted to help you become aware of the patterns of Blamespeak, so that you do not get hooked into using Blamespeak yourself. Of course, no one is perfect, but the more you avoid Blamespeak yourself, the calmer and more productive your coparenting communication can be. Remember, sometimes the other coparent will respond in a similar manner once they have seen several of your carefully-written BIFF communications. However, some people use Blamespeak and will never change. In either case, how you communicate will help you and your child or children find more moments of peace regardless of how your coparent communicates.

The next chapter explains the four basic ingredients of a BIFF communication, using coparenting examples. The rest of this book will give you examples of BIFF communications for many specific coparenting situations. We will teach you how to choose your words carefully.

# CHAPTER TWO

# Writing a BIFF Communication

BIFF communications (or "BIFFs") are usually in writing, including emails, texts, social media posts and even written notes and letters. They can also be used in person; however, we have a separate book *(Calming Upset People with EAR)* designed specifically for calming in-person conversations using *EAR Statements,* which are briefly described in Appendix C. But it's actually good to learn to use BIFF communications first.

**BIFF stands for:**

B RIEF

I NFORMATIVE

F RIENDLY

F IRM

This may seem easy, but it's actually harder than you may think at first. You have to restrain yourself from firing back with Blamespeak. With practice, the BIFF formula will work for you. Of course, when you receive a Blamespeak email or other communication, it helps to step back for a moment at least and not respond right away.

# BIFF for CoParent Communication

Here's a short description of each step of a BIFF:

**BRIEF**

Your communication should be very short, such as one paragraph of 2-5 sentences in most cases. It doesn't matter how long the Blamespeak statement is that you are responding to; your response should be short. The point is to avoid triggering defensiveness in the other person. You are going to do your best to focus that person on problem-solving information. To do this, don't give too many words for the other person to react to. The more you say, the more likely you are to trigger another Blamespeak response, which doesn't do your children any good.

Keeping it brief isn't easy. It is highly recommended that whenever possible, you give your proposed BIFF response to someone else to review before it is sent out. A reviewer who is familiar with the BIFF process will almost always trim it down and that usually makes it better.

**INFORMATIVE**

Give a sentence or two of straight, useful information on the subject being discussed. With a coparent, this is usually straightforward information about an activity, a doctor visit, a school issue, or passing on some information you've gotten from a third party. It may be notification of the child's illness, or notification of upcoming travel. If there is no real subject or issue (because the Blamespeak communication you received is simply angry and venting), you can still give some related helpful information. Your response can shift the discussion to an objective subject, rather than opinions about each other's personality. It's important to not include anything in the response that includes your opinion, or any defensiveness about the subject. Just provide straight information, presented in neutral terms, as briefly as possible.

### FRIENDLY

Friendly is often the hardest part, but it's very important. You can start with something like: "Thank you for telling me your opinion on this subject." Or: "I appreciate your concerns." Or just: "Thanks for your email. Here is some information you may not have . . . . " You can also end your response with a friendly comment, no matter how hard that might seem! An example: "I hope you have a nice weekend."

### FIRM

The goal of most of your BIFF responses with your coparent is to end the conversation. This is the case if you're trying to disengage from a potentially high-conflict situation initiated by the other parent. You want to let the other parent know that this is all you are going to say on the subject. Then you have to stick to that resolution. In some cases, you will give two clear choices for future action, which would require an additional response from the coparent. If you need a response, then it will help to set a firm, reasonable reply date. If you are going to take action if the other parent does not do something, then you could say, for example: "If I don't receive the information I need by [reasonable date], then I will have to do [your action]. I would prefer to have your input." (Note that this is both firm and friendly.) Also note that in general, asking for a response or input in a very short time is usually not reasonable, and your request for another response should give at least 24-48 hours unless that's simply not possible.

## It's Not What You Feel Like Doing

Of course, BIFF responses are often not what you feel like doing. You don't want to be friendly to someone who is attacking you. You may hate each of the steps described above. You may feel more like being abusive right back to the other parent. Responding with Blamespeak is more satisfying and feels much stronger. Or you might feel like withdrawing, hiding, and having no contact with the other parent, although this usually is not realistically possible.

The reality is that Blamespeak gives you a very brief high, much like a drug. The high vanishes when the other person responds with more Blamespeak, and you're left with that sickening, fearful or angry feeling inside again. Or, the other parent will share your Blamespeak with third parties, people who may be important to you or your child, and who could affect the third party's opinion of you. Or, you will now have to explain yourself even more to them, and the third party (whether a child's teacher, or a family court judge) won't have full background about "who started it."

BIFF responses don't usually give you a high. But they can give you a sense of relief, the satisfaction that you acted as the grown-up in a situation, and they can end a high-conflict discussion. They may even solve a problem.

## Do You Need to Respond?

In many cases, it's better not to respond at all. Here's some Blamespeak you can generally ignore:

- When no one else is or will be involved in the communication except you and the other person.

- When there is clearly no real issue being discussed. They are simply venting at you, and their personality is the issue.

- When it is simply the other person's opinion about your behavior or personality. Responding to them will not change their opinion.

- When it is clear that you will not change the other person's point of view.

- When you have already responded previously and sufficiently on the same subject.

## When to Respond with a BIFF

In general, it's best to respond promptly but not immediately (catch your breath first), and to have your response reviewed by someone else, if possible. Prompt responses are important for three reasons:

- Blamespeakers tend to believe that you agree with their opinions of you unless you disagree fairly quickly. Unfortunately, silence means consent in their defensive ways of thinking.

- Blamespeakers often tell other people about all the bad things they perceive you have done. If other people don't hear that you disagree, then the HCP's comments could be assumed true by the other people involved. These types of communications with third parties, such as the child's teachers or health providers, are specifically discussed later in this book.

- Blamespeakers are so emotionally intense that their statements may sound and feel true. (Emotions are contagious and *intense* emotions are *intensely* contagious.) So, their *emotions* often persuade others that you are acting badly and that the Blamespeaker is your victim, unless you can quickly inform them with factual information that overrides and counters the emotions.

For example:

Blamespeaker: "Father never responded to my request. I was left hanging for weeks and it cost me a lot."

This statement isn't true because Father did respond. But without a response, it sounds true, and influences the listener's opinion of the target of the blame. If Father hasn't responded quickly, the statement becomes a given fact, and other's opinions become established about you.

## To Whom Should You Respond?

Generally, we recommend that you respond to the same person or people in the same format used by the Blamespeaker. If it was an email or letter from the other parent to you, then you can respond by email, if you determine a response is even necessary. If the communication was copied to another person (family friend, teacher, lawyer, coach, etc.), then you should usually include that third party in your response. If it was sent to a group of people (all soccer team parents), then strongly consider responding to the group—such as using Reply All with an email—so that you don't risk that someone will believe the Blamespeak about you in the absence of your response.

## What is your Goal?

There are usually three goals to consider with your coparent:

**To manage the coparenting relationship**, for the benefit of your children. You have no choice but to make this relationship work somehow.

**To reduce the relationship** to a less intense level, such as a parallel parenting relationship with the other parent, with as little direct communication between the two of you as possible. A well-structured Parenting Plan that has specifics covering almost all situations with your children will assist a lot in reducing the relationship to its bare bones. Court-ordered technology, such as limiting all communications to emails, such as Our Family Wizard, Peaceful Parent, an online calendar, or ProperComm, and others can be helpful to reduce the relationship.

**To end the relationship.** While this is sometimes an option with someone who is not a coparent, this is usually not an option with the coparent. This drastic option is sometimes necessary with other relatives involved in the coparent's life.

How you communicate with your coparent will make a big difference, especially if they engage in a lot of Blamespeak. If you inadvertently give him or her negative feedback, you may increase the intensity of their interactions with you, as many people can't handle negative feedback. The use of BIFF will assist with this, as one tenet of BIFF is that you stick to current information and that you do not blame or rehash the past. In some instances, when explaining your concerns about the past is absolutely necessary to resolving an issue, remind yourself to follow the BIFF process. It's always preferable to place emphasis on the *desired future behavior*. To do this, you may have to acknowledge the past somehow. Just keep the focus on the future as much as possible.

If your statements are too rejecting, such as statements about suddenly reducing the frequency and type of communications with you, the other person is likely to *increase* interactions with you, and the intensity of their emotions. There may be threats of punishment against you for limiting the relationship, and possibly accusations of "not coparenting" or being a terrible parent.

Because sudden changes cause escalation, we recommend reducing or *phasing out* relationships when necessary, as people need time to process and accept change. Otherwise, when changes are too abrupt, they may try to assert control by stalking, harassing, or even suing you. Remember, a Blamespeaker usually does not realize his or her actions are unreasonable or that anything is their fault, so they may seek the court's assistance to prove that you're not coparenting correctly.

As a coparent, your best option is to reduce, but continue, your relationship with the other parent at a less intense level. The shared interest—your children—will always remain, hopefully while avoiding the most negative aspects of the communications. There are very, very few cases where a family court can permit a parent to cut off all contact with the other parent. Some level of coparenting contact and communication will be necessary for as long as the children are dependent on you both.

Whatever your ultimate goal with the other parent, keep it in mind when interacting (or avoiding interacting), to always give a BIFF response. Before every interaction, ask yourself: Will my response engage the other parent more in my life? Will the response allow him or her to back off without defensiveness? Throughout the examples in this book, you will see that the main goal is avoidance of triggering the other parent's defensiveness, while also exchanging information and making decisions that benefit your children.

## A School Example

(Examples are based on real-life parenting decisions, entirely altered to respect privacy.)

> (Nathan) What does Jaylen need for school dress-up day on Friday?

(Ashley) You're such an idiot. The school sent home a whole flyer about dress-up day. If you had a brain in your head, you'd read things from the school and wouldn't have to ask me stupid questions. You've never done anything a good parent would do and Jaylen always suffers for it.

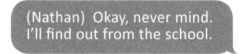

(Nathan) Look who's talking. The great mother who forgot to pick up her son from school twice last semester, and left him standing on the curb by himself for an hour.

But suppose that Nathan decided to use a BIFF response to Ashley's Blamespeak *instead* of what he wrote above. Would the following be a good response? Would it be a BIFF?

(Nathan) Okay, never mind. I'll find out from the school.

## BIFF CHECKER — Is this a BIFF?

**Did he consider whether he needed to respond?**

☑ Yes
☐ No
☐ Maybe

Suppose that Nathan just didn't respond and decided to go somewhere else for the information. He could decide to calm things down and end it for now. He didn't want to just end the conversation with Ashley's insults, because that might make Ashley think she had *won* or intimidated him. If he also didn't want to over-react with Blamespeak himself, the response "Never mind" was appropriate.

**Brief?**  ☑ **Yes**
☐ No
☐ Maybe

His response was very brief, but sufficient for his goal.

**Informative?**  ☑ **Yes**
☐ No
☐ Maybe

Because Nathan said he would ask the school, he has kept the focus on his original question. He lets Ashley know he was seeking information and that's all. He totally avoids responding to everything else Ashley said.

**Friendly?**  ☐ Yes
☐ No
☑ **Maybe**

Somewhat, because he said "Okay." This is friendly enough, by not ignoring her completely. He could have said "Thanks for responding to my question," but this would have sounded sarcastic, since Ashley's 's response was so insulting. When there's this much Blamespeak, it's best to just say "okay" and move on.

**Firm?**  ☑ **Yes**
☐ No
☐ Maybe

Firm enough. Nathan ended the conversation. He gave Ashley nothing else to respond to.

In this next example, there's enough history to show that one person has a *pattern* of high-conflict behavior, so it's especially important to use a BIFF.

## A Schedule Example

(Victor) Once again you've asked me for a favor in changing the parenting time, and it's not going to happen. You are constantly doing this, but you never want to give me any extra time—you only take. You think you control everything but you don't seem to get it that I have equal parenting time and equal decision-making with you. READ THE COURT ORDERS, idiot. No, you can't have the kids on my time.

(Hannah) Thank you for responding to my request to take the children to my family reunion. I probably didn't mention that their cousins from Nebraska will be there, and as you know, they love their cousins and would have liked to see them. Since you do not agree, then of course I will respect that and withdraw my request, as I recognize it is your parenting time.

# BIFF CHECKER

---

**Did Hannah consider whether she needed to respond?**

☑ Yes
☐ No
☐ Maybe

Because this was just between them, she didn't have to respond, but responding with a BIFF often calms things more than no response. Since she had made a scheduling request, she needed to let him know that she had received Victor's response and that she was withdrawing her request. Otherwise, she could probably have ignored his email altogether. She didn't need to respond to his accusations and insults, so she ignored those parts of the email. Hannah kept it brief and avoided the urge to defend herself.

---

**Brief?**

☑ Yes
☐ No
☐ Maybe

It was just one paragraph with three sentences.

---

**Informative?**

☑ Yes
☐ No
☐ Maybe

There are basically two sentences of information about her request, and they were neutral and objective. She added information that the children's cousins would be present.

This shifted some of the focus from evaluating each other to evaluating details (something important for the children). Importantly, she did not spend any time countering his allegations against her. There was no need, as she will not change his mind. She doesn't need to defend herself that she has in fact read their Parenting Plan; it would just renew the argument. She was able to avoid getting emotionally hooked into defending herself unnecessarily.

---

**Friendly?**     ☑ **Yes**
              ☐ No
              ☐ Maybe

She said "Thank you for responding..." "Since you do not agree, then of course I will respect that..."

---

**Firm?**      ☑ **Yes**
              ☐ No
              ☐ Maybe

She ended the discussion. Her request is withdrawn and there's nothing more to say about it. While she repeated her belief that it would be a good experience for the children, she did not leave it as an open question. If he changes his mind based on the new information, she will be happy about that, but she does not expect it. She is realistic and not asking him again. If she asked him again, after making her "informative" statement, she might just be opening herself up to another personal attack. So, she has closed the discussion. (Nothing in her email prevents him from writing back and saying he changed his mind, but she knows this is highly unlikely given their history.)

**Alternative Firm response:** If she thought he might change his mind after receiving her information, she could have said: "With this information, I hope you will reconsider. Please let me know Yes or No by Thursday at 5pm."

This would also be a firm response because it is just asking for a Yes or No answer, without opening up another argument. It really depends on whether she thinks he might change his mind with the new information. If not, then it may be pointless to ask this question. It's always a judgment call for the BIFF writer.

**Comment about others copied on an email:** What if Victor had copied his email to friends or other family members (which Blamespeakers often do), then we recommend that Hannah should respond to the same group with more information, such as the following:

> (Hannah) Dear friends and family: As you know, Victor and I had a difficult divorce. He has sent you a private text showing correspondence between us about a parenting schedule matter. I hope you will see this as a private matter and understand that you do not need to respond or get involved in any way. Almost everything he has said is in anger and not at all accurate. If you have any questions for me personally, please feel free to contact me and I will clarify anything I can. I appreciate your friendship and support.

And that's it: BIFF! A key point here is that she didn't counter each individual allegation of Victor's. Instead, she replied "Almost everything he has said is in anger and not at all accurate." That takes care of it. Now everyone knows she does not agree with him. Nothing is left unchallenged. If anyone wants more information, they can contact her. Usually, family and friends are happy to stay out of it and leave them alone. Very importantly, Hannah is not the one who included the third parties in the original correspondence, which they probably appreciate.

**Additional note about reviewing your own BIFF:** Do you think the "in anger" sentence is even necessary: "Almost everything he has said is in anger and not at all accurate." If you go back and read this paragraph without that sentence it actually makes the point anyway and perhaps makes it stronger because she is briefer and not focusing on his behavior. By leaving out this sentence, Hannah is simply saying the others don't need to get involved, but she can clarify anything if they have questions. This appears to make it clear that she does not feel she has to defend anything.

**Writing tip:** When you're preparing a BIFF communication, if you have a sentence you're not sure about, simply read the BIFF paragraph out loud with the sentence and then read it again without the sentence. See which one sounds better to you.

**More than one possible BIFF:** This example shows that with or without that sentence, it is still a BIFF response. There's often more than one reasonable way to write a BIFF. It really depends on three things:

1. The BIFF writer
2. The BIFF reader, and
3. The situation surrounding the BIFF communication.

Just remember to keep it Brief, Informative, Friendly and Firm.

# Conclusion

This chapter gave you the key four ingredients of a BIFF communication for any coparenting situation. Here we had two examples of using a BIFF response to hostility. Keep it Brief, Informative, Friendly and Firm. It's not as easy as it sounds, but with practice and by checking your BIFFs with someone you trust, you will get better and better at it. The hardest part is seeing personal allegations about yourself and understanding that you don't need to respond to those attacks. It is possible to respond and avoid Blamespeak.

The next chapter tells you how to avoid the most common mistakes people make in their BIFFs.

# CHAPTER THREE

# Avoid the 3 A's: Admonishments, Advice and Apologies

In responding to Blamespeak emails, it's nearly impossible to resist the urge to write blamespeak back. Personal attacks are hard to ignore. We see models on a daily basis of people on television fighting back and arguing about things said about them. It's called drama, and that draws us in. We are wired, as humans, to respond to attacks against us. **Blamespeak triggers the defensive part of your brain.** Before we explain the details of avoiding Blamespeak in your BIFFs, we will explain a little about why our brains have such a hard time with this. This brief explanation should make it easier for you to overcome the powerful urge to slip Blamespeak into your BIFFs.

## Your Brain in a Conflict

Our brains are really a combination of parts that serve different purposes. They take turns in dominating our thinking at times and generally work together—just as we have many muscles in our arms that work together rather than just one muscle.

Our brains are very flexible and the location of brain activity for different purposes varies somewhat person to person. Our comments about the brain throughout this book are based on reading research, attending seminars, and seeing what works in the practice of conflict resolution. This book is meant to be practical and general, rather than scientifically exact.

The two main response methods in our brains for dealing with conflict generally operate as follows:

1. **Fast defensive reacting.** This brain function can respond in less than a tenth of a second, to get us out of a bad situation before we even start to "think" about it. It's probably saved your life many times (almost falling off a cliff, escaping a bully, a run-away car, a flood, etc.), especially when you were a young child.

   It's an action-oriented response, so it doesn't have time or energy for analyzing situations. In fact, when upset enough, the *amygdala* shuts down our logical thinking. It focuses on a fight, flight or freeze response, that sees people and situations in all-or-nothing terms, that jumps to conclusions and is driven by intense emotional energy (especially the energy of fear and anger). The amygdala acts like a smoke alarm—it gets all of your attention and doesn't leave room for slowly thinking things through.

2. **Logical problem-solving.** This brain is much more accurate in analyzing problems— when there's time and

it isn't shut off by the amygdala. This brain can look into the past objectively and compare the present situation in depth, to see how similar and how different it is.

This function of the brain can take the time to plan logical responses to a situation and consider the distant future consequences, which the defensive parts of the brain don't have time for in a crisis or life-threatening conflict.

Some think of the brain as primarily having language skills and logical problem-solving, which are generally associated with the left hemisphere of the brain, while intense and negative emotions are mostly processed in the right brain. But frankly, where these happen in the brain is less important than understanding how to manage your own thinking in a conflict.

Most of the time, we as adults use our logical problem-solving thinking. But when a situation feels threatening enough or totally new, our defensive reacting can take over and shut down our logical problem-solving. Sound familiar? Can you remember when you last experienced this?

As children grow up and become adults, they become more able to tell the difference between a crisis and a minor disagreement or problem. In fact, this is one of the main tasks of adolescence: to learn how to deal with major crises, minor crises, and what isn't a crisis at all. This comes from millions of experiences, as neurons are constantly growing connections in our brains, associating problems in life to our successful strategies for solving similar problems in the past. Much of this wisdom becomes stored in our brains for future use.

## Talking to the "Right" Brain

Blamespeak, in particular, seems to trigger our fast defensive brain response, as it is often interpreted as a crisis, stopping our logical thinking and making us agitated to get ready for action. This makes sense, because Blamespeak is a personal attack, even if it's just a verbal attack. When exposed to the intensity of Blamespeak, we can easily get emotionally hooked into defending ourselves.

But logically there's no need to defend yourself in response to Blamespeak, because *it's not about you.* It's about the person who can't control himself or herself. You don't have to prove anything. But emotionally it's hard (but possible) to override personal attacks.

We have to train ourselves to remember *during a high-conflict moment* that it's really about the Blamespeaker's inability to manage his or her own emotions and behavior. So, we can switch ourselves back to our logical problem-solving left brains. There's often no action we need to take at all. Of course, you may need to take action to protect yourself if there is a physical or legal threat. But you don't need to defend your own actions or prove who you are as a person to any Blamespeaker. Blamespeak is on them.

## You Can Retrain Your Brain

Brain scientists have learned that you can change your own brain by practicing learning skills. You can even learn to do the opposite of what you once did, if you practice enough. That's how it is with writing BIFF responses. Even though you may feel tempted to write a Blamespeak response, you can train yourself to weed out the Blamespeak and just write a pure BIFF. You'll be amazed at how well you can do.

You can train yourself to think, feel and say to yourself: "His comments are not really about me." "The issue's not the issue." "Her personality is the issue." And other short, quick sayings that train your brain to not react defensively.

With practice, you can keep yourself from slipping over into *fight, flight or freeze* or, if you get emotionally hooked, to bring yourself back fairly quickly. We have been teaching this skill for years and still get emotionally hooked sometimes—but catch ourselves much quicker than we used to. Then we can usually bring ourselves back to being logical and calm again. Writing BIFFs can really help you with that. It helps you focus on writing carefully, rather than emotionally reacting.

You can also influence the other person's response to you. If you can respond calmly, it actually helps the other person manage their own fearful or angry response. In many ways, you can decide if the other person will react defensively or think logically about what you say—all based on your ability to send a BIFF instead of Blamespeak.

## #1: Avoid Admonishments

Admonishments are personal criticisms by a person in a superior role, such as a parent or a judge. Admonishments between coparents often feel like a personal attack and trigger defensive reacting for the reasons explained above.

For example, you might feel like saying to your coparent "You should know better than this." "I'm surprised you would even consider this" "Look in the mirror, Jorge." These are examples of comments that might sound innocent to the person giving the admonishment, but to most listeners, they sound judgmental and insulting. These expressions aren't conducive to BIFF responses, as they don't provide information and they aren't friendly.

The message of an admonishment is that you are superior to the person you are writing to and have the right to criticize their behavior. It's the assumption that you can judge the other person's behavior that feels the most offensive. The response to admonishments is likely to be defensive, as the responder tries to justify their own actions and probably blame you back even more so. Instead, try to avoid triggering this defensiveness and stay focused on the four elements of a BIFF response. These elements are designed to help you avoid slipping into admonishments.

## #2: Avoid Advice

Giving advice creates the same problem as admonishments, even if it feels neutral. "But I'm just trying to help with a few suggestions!" You may think it's *constructive feedback*, but if the person didn't ask you for feedback or suggestions, then you are treating the person disrespectfully, as if you are in a superior position to him. This is likely to trigger a defensive response and counter-attack. It helps to remember that some Blamespeakers spend a lot of their day in defensiveness, and you shouldn't reinforce this tendency by giving unwanted advice.

One big problem in communications between coparents is that when your relationship was intact, or at least better, the other person may have wanted and asked for your advice, so you're used to giving suggestions. Unfortunately, with the end of the relationship, your coparent may no longer want your advice, and now views *advice* as meddling. It's tough to recognize that the relationship has changed.

If you want to feel out the other person's receptiveness to suggestions or advice, simply add "The soccer club website has a lot of information, but please feel free to ask me anything you need to know about the upcoming tournament." This is friendly, gives information (there's a soccer website!) and leaves the decision about whether advice is wanted or not in your coparent's hands.

Other family members and friends may be another source of unwanted advice—giving or receiving—especially as you are going through a separation or divorce. It's very tempting to want to give them advice. "Look, Mom, let me give you some advice about this situation . . ." Just hold back on sharing that thought. It will save you a lot of unnecessary conflict.

Likewise, it's common that adult children and their parents slip into trying to give each other advice in their own relationship. "Look, Dad, I can handle my own career planning. In fact, let me give you some friendly advice about your situation." Once again, it's better to hold back on your own advice-giving, in exchange for protecting yourself from the advice of others. Especially when there's angry emails or texts, it is no time for giving *friendly* advice.

If you desperately want to give someone advice, ask them if they would like a suggestion. If they say "Yes," then you can feel free. But if they say "No," you're better off leaving it alone.

# #3: Avoid Apologies

Avoiding apologies might be the opposite of what you would expect. Shouldn't I offer apologies to make the other parent feel better? While apologies are helpful with many situations, they often backfire with someone who is looking for a fight. Instead of thanking you for your apology and ending the issue, a coparent who is difficult will very possibly interpret an apology in an all-or-nothing manner. An apology can be interpreted as an admission that you agree "It's all my fault." That will reinforce their belief that everything really is all your fault and they will remind you of this the next time there is a different conflict (and the next time, and the next time!).

It takes people (including the authors) quite a while to figure this out about apologies. Bill recounts an instance in a counseling session where the husband, quite a bully, pulled out an ancient written apology from the wife and used it against her in counseling, even though it obviously was a long-past attempt to placate him. He wanted to use her apology as current evidence that he was right about everything, and she was wrong—and admitted in writing that she was wrong. When sent to someone with no self-awareness and an ability to take on any blame, apologies can simply be misused. They reinforce all-or-nothing belief systems.

Simple apologies like "I'm sorry I'm late" or "I'm sorry we couldn't agree" may be okay as social niceties. But even be careful about using the word "sorry," because you can't control how they hear it and interpret it. In many situations, it may be better to use the word "saddened." "I'm *saddened* to see we're in this situation" can show empathy, without appearing to take blame for the situation.

In short, watch out for the "3 A's" described above whenever you write a BIFF. As always, having a third party double-check your writings is a plus.

Here's an example of a coparent exchange:

## A Sorry Example

> (Savannah) I can't believe you did this again! Your daughter was the last person to be picked up from soccer because YOU FORGOT her and you were probably off with that stupid girlfriend of yours. Alexa is so embarrassed, and her coach had to wait with her at least a half hour after all the other girls had left. She's going to just refuse to come to your house at all, and she KNOWS I'm the only person she can rely on."

> (Omar) I'm so sorry. I got caught up at work and lost all track of time. I texted Alexa and her coach as soon as I realized what I'd done, and they both said they understood and would wait. I promise this won't happen again, and I apologized to Alexa.

> (Savannah) You're SORRY?
> For being a rotten parent?
> Some things are way more
> important than sorry. Saying
> you're sorry doesn't make up
> for being a horrible person
> and parent.

## BIFF CHECKER

---

**Did Omar consider if he needed to respond?**

☑ **Yes**
☐ No
☐ Maybe

As picking up a child late is pretty important, this communication from Mother did need a response.

---

**Brief?**

☐ Yes
☑ **No**
☐ Maybe

The response is a little longer than it needed to be, and Omar overdid the extent of his apology (which, after all, should be directed more to his daughter than to the coparent).

---

**Informative?**

☐ Yes
☑ **No**
☐ Maybe

Again, a little too much information is given.

**Friendly?**  ☐ Yes
☐ No
☑ Maybe

It's friendly, and maybe a little too much so.

**Firm?**  ☐ Yes
☑ **No**
☐ Maybe

It's not very firm. It does not adequately put a stop to communication on this issue.

**Did Omar double-check for admonishments, advice, or apologies?** No, he didn't. His apology was overdone and Savannah is using it against him and saying it isn't good enough. She will remember this and probably bring it up over and over again.

**What's a better way of writing Omar's response?**

> (Omar) I regret that this happened. I have apologized to Alexa. It won't happen again.

This way he doesn't feed the word "sorry" to Savannah to use against him in the future. If he had said "I'm sorry this happened," it might be taken as a social nicety, but it's always a risk. The effect on the child is acknowledged. The response is firm and does not invite further discussion.

# Use and Abuse of Social Media by Coparents

Facebook and other social media offer the opportunity to communicate with many people at once. This can be a good thing. However, it also offers every single one of a coparent's Facebook Friends a chance to see comments about a parent and respond immediately for all to see. Blamespeak is rampant on social media.

Even when a parent posts something initially innocuous, responders, including difficult coparents or a third party, might respond with a personal attack. An all-out war can erupt between two or more commenters in a matter of minutes, with other commenters taking sides. People who don't even know each other join in. All of this escalates rapidly.

You've likely heard the term "troll" as describing those on Facebook or other social media who seem to be online only to stir up problems. Wikipedia defines "internet troll" as "a person who starts quarrels or upsets people on the internet to distract and sow discord by posting inflammatory and digressive, extraneous, or off-topic messages in an online community . . . with the intent of provoking readers into displaying emotional responses . . . whether for the troll's amusement or a specific gain." Trolls will enjoy getting involved in a coparenting issue because trolls are always looking for discord.

Fortunately, a BIFF response online can clear up an issue, or at least can start to de-escalate it. The more that people use BIFF responses online, the more the Blamespeakers will stand out as being the exception rather than the norm.

People *can* learn to catch themselves and respond with

BIFFs—or not respond at all. As explained earlier in this chapter, the amygdala in your brain can get emotionally hooked, but we can override the fear and anger responses by practicing reasonable responses like BIFFs. A friend on social media can also help by stepping in and giving a BIFF to help reduce the conflict. As people learn more about Blamespeak, they may be less likely to want to use it themselves. Aware friends who see what's going on and understand BIFF can avoid getting hooked and adding to the Blamespeak.

# Conclusion

Responding to Blamespeak—or any difficult situation—with a BIFF can be harder than you think. By learning BIFF, you are training your brain to think in a new way, and to overcome immediate *fight* impulses when you're attacked. The retraining process is one reason it's helpful to have someone else review your communications and responses before you send them. What you leave out of your communications is just as important (maybe more important) than what you say.

The next several chapters give examples of many different coparenting BIFF situations. Difficult coparents tend to focus on the other parent, or the other parent's family and friends, as their *targets of blame*. The next chapters are about using BIFFs with common coparenting issues.

An added bonus is that in learning to write effective communication with your coparent, you will find the same skills apply to your communications with friends, family, coworkers, neighbors, and difficult people you'll encounter in all walks of life.

# SECTION

2

# CHAPTER FOUR

# BIFFs About Routine Coparenting

Divorced or separated coparents come from several types of relationships. Some couples were married for years and have a substantial history together. Others were married or together for a very short time, and still other coparents barely know each other. It's impossible to say which type of former relationship makes for the best or worst coparenting relationships, but it's safe to say that if one or both parents use a lot of Blamespeak, the coparenting relationship will be difficult.

**A Few Words on Gatekeeping.** Coparenting communications shouldn't be discussed without a mention of gatekeeping. Gatekeeping means that one parent or the other is more in control of information about the child, or has more control of the child himself. How that parent (the "gatekeeper") controls or manages the child's relationship with the other parent can be a big point of conflict between parents. In intact relationships, gatekeeping is often intentionally practiced by the family. One parent may be "in charge" of most child information and day-to-day issues for the family. That parent may be the one who knows all the child's teachers and medical providers, is responsible for all the phone calls to caretakers, and takes the children to all their appointments and activities. That gatekeeper parent may report to the other parent about what's going on (or the other parent may not need or want a report), and the parents may be perfectly happy with their unequal status when it comes to the children, because that arrangement works well within the family.

When the parents then separate, that unequal arrangement can suddenly feel harsh and unfair to the non-controlling parent. The gatekeeper parent may feel the status quo should be maintained for the benefit of the child. This tension in post-separation gatekeeping often leads to difficult communications. Both the former gatekeeper and the former non-gatekeeper need to be aware of the changes they both must make. Changing the nature of what was a long-standing parenting relationship doesn't happen immediately.

## A Gatekeeping Example

Holly and Ryan were married for 8 years and have two young children. They both work hard outside the home but Holly has always been responsible for dealing with the children's caretakers and schools and making teacher and pediatrician appointments. Ryan knew Holly was doing a good job with this and trusted her to handle everything. They are now separated and Ryan's girlfriend can't believe that Ryan isn't more hands-on with his children. "Why does she get to take the children to all their doctor's appointments? Don't you care what's going on with them? She shouldn't get to do all those things. She just takes and takes, and then sends you the bills." As the result of his girlfriend's insistence (she may be a bit of a Blamespeaker herself), Ryan starts asking to do some of these things for the children:

> **(Ryan)** It's not fair that you take the children to all their appointments and do all the talking to the teachers for both of us. I'm an equal parent and should be taking them to at least half their doctor's appointments. I shouldn't have to hear from you that Brianna needs braces—I should be able to talk directly with the dentist. From now on, I'll be taking the kids to every other appointment with Dr. Spreck and the dentist, Dr. Moore.

Holly, who was not happy about the divorce, does not want to give up her status as gatekeeper of the children's information and contacts. She has developed some Blamespeak as the result of the girlfriend's involvement.

> **(Holly)** You are such an idiot! I've been doing all the doctor's appointments and handling the kids' routines since they were born. For seven years I did everything, and suddenly you think you're going to be able to do those things as well? I know it's your ridiculous girlfriend who wants to pretend like she's their Mom and show up at appointments! That slut is not going to my kids' appointments. You're such a fool and everyone at school is making fun of your new "relationship" and talking about you behind your back. I'm sure you think you'll be a happy little family with

that woman but you'll take my kids to appointments over my dead body. If she shows her face at our doctor or at Luke's soccer games, she will regret it.

Now Ryan is faced with how to respond. He has equal parenting time and equal decision-making with Holly but Holly won't give up any of her authority. How can he give a BIFF response and move the discussion forward in a productive way?

> **(Ryan)** We have joint legal decision-making [custody] for our children. We both want what's best for them and we both want to be involved. Our parenting documents point out that we're both supposed to do these things. I contacted Dr. Spreck's office and found out that the next scheduled appointment for Brianna is on March 14. As that's on your parenting day, I will change that appointment to the next one available on my parenting day so that I can take her. I will let you know of the new appointment date and will email you about everything the doctor says.

## BIFF CHECKER

Brief?  ☑ Yes
 ☐ No
 ☐ Maybe

Somewhat. The length of his email is probably okay as he needed to point Holly to their parenting documents as backup for what he wants to do.

**Informative?**   ☑ **Yes**
              ☐ No
              ☐ Maybe

He specifically told her what he is going to do with the next appointment and he made reference to their parenting documents.

**Friendly?**    **Yes**
              ☐ No
              ☐ Maybe

His tone was friendly and he didn't make reference to Holly's insults or his girlfriend. Holly tried to get him into a fight by insulting his girlfriend but Ryan didn't take the bait. His intent here is taking his kids to their appointments, not defending his girlfriend's honor.

**Firm?**   ☑ **Yes**
              ☐ No
              ☐ Maybe

He's stated a specific plan of action about the March 14 doctor appointment and made it clear how he's going to handle it.

**Advice?**   ☐ Yes
               **No**
              ☐ Maybe

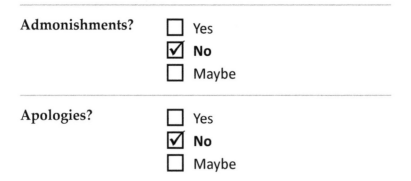

It can also be the case that the previously intact family always had a parent who was dependent on the rest of the family to solve his or her routine daily life problems. After separation, this parent may angrily blame their former partner, and even the children, when they don't continue to do what the more dependent parent wants or if they make that parent's life more difficult. Using BIFF responses can be part of managing this type of family problem as the structure of the family changes to one of more equal responsibility.

**BIFF It Again:** Did you spot any issues in Ryan's response that would upset Holly? His approach may feel too aggressive for some coparenting situations as he unilaterally changed the doctor's appointment that Holly unilaterally made, potentially adding fuel to the fire. It's a good idea to keep BIFF'ing your response to remove any of your own Blamespeak or any unintended landmines. The goal is to contain the conflict, not escalate it. Here is Ryan's second pass at BIFF'ing his response:

> **(Ryan)** We have joint legal decision-making [custody] for our children. We both want what's best for them and we both want to be involved. Our parenting

documents point out that we're both supposed to do these things. I contacted Dr. Spreck's office about Brianna's next scheduled appointment, which is March 14 on one of your parenting days. The next time she needs to go to the doctor, I will schedule it on one of my parenting days so that I can take her. I will let you know of the new appointment date and will email you about everything the doctor says afterward.

Rather than undoing what Holly had done, he is asserting himself about making the next appointment. Which BIFF is better? Remember, it depends on:

The BIFF writer

The BIFF reader, and

The situation surrounding the BIFF communication.

As long as the communication is Brief, Informative, Friendly and Firm, and avoid the 3 A's, it should help address the situation in a relatively calm but firm manner.

## A Dance Lesson Example

Rashon and Tamika were married for fifteen years and had three children together. Rashon has been known to be difficult throughout his life. Over the years, Tamika and the children learned to manage Rashon's moods and cater to him when he was upset. Now that Tamika has filed for divorce, Rashon gradually catches on that not only is he losing half of his assets, Tamika is no longer available to pay his bills and manage daily life for him. Rashon requested 50% parenting time with the children, which the court awarded despite the fact that he rarely spent time with them during the marriage, nor did he handle much of the children's needs such as extracurricular activities and medical appointments.

Tamika, like Holly above, found it difficult to give up the responsibilities she managed for the children throughout their lives. Not surprisingly, she was not happy that Rashon got nearly 50% parenting time as he doesn't know how to occupy them, feed them, or get them to their activities. When she sees the children miss out on things while with their father, she feels guilty and angry. Why should the children miss out on things? Their communications about the children are not productive. Tamika chastises Rashon that he didn't get their youngest to her dance lesson, and none of the children had lunches for school on his parenting days.

> **(Tamika)** You demanded to have them half the time! You need to make sure they have everything they need! Shanda missed her dance lesson, which I'm sure she told you about in advance. And both kids told me you didn't prepare school lunches for them.

Rashon, on the other hand, had in his mind that no one told him about the dance lesson, and that lunch was provided for the children at school.

> **(Rashon)** You just don't get it! You need to tell me when Shanda has a lesson and you need to tell me when the kids need school lunches and what they'll eat. You withhold all the information about the kids just to set me up and make me look like a loser dad and to make the kids hate me.

Let's try this again with a BIFF communication on Tamika's part. Remember, you can start a conversation using the BIFF method just as easily as you can use a BIFF to respond. Her first email above was not effective, and she's still disappointed that the children might miss out on things, but she's ready to do better, without completely running Rashon's life for him.

> **(Tamika)** I agree it's important that we both know the children's schedules. I suggest we set up a shared online calendar where all the schedules can be posted. The children's lunch accounts are available on their school website under "Lunch Program." This tab shows you if the children have money in their hot lunch accounts. The login information for the school accounts is at the end of this email.

## BIFF CHECKER

**Brief?**
☐ Yes
☐ No
☑ Maybe

Kind of. It has a lot of information.

**Informative?**
☑ **Yes**
☐ No
☐ Maybe

Very. It has maybe a little too much information for one email.

**Friendly?**  ☑ Yes
☐ No
☐ Maybe

She agreed with someone Rashon intimated rather than attack him.

**Firm?**  ☑ Yes
☐ No
☐ Maybe

She made a specific request for a shared calendar.

**Advice?**  ☐ Yes
☐ No
☑ Maybe

Her suggestion about a shared calendar appears to be helpful but Rashon may take it as advice.

**Admonishments?**  ☐ Yes
☑ No
☐ Maybe

**Apologies?**  ☐ Yes
☑ No
☐ Maybe

**A response date?** When making a request in a BIFF communication, it often helps to ask for a response date. In Tamika's email she said "I suggest we set up a shared calendar...." She could have said, "Please let me know by Friday if you agree, so we can set it up this weekend." However, as with all BIFF communications, she might prefer to leave it up in the air as a suggestion and see if he responds. Asking for a response date is often based on how urgent a response is needed.

**Use of distraction:** Tamika could also use a method that sometimes works with upset people in a BIFF communication: She could distract Rashon from his immediate anger with a helpful or friendly comment about something else. In this case, she suggested a shared online calendar that would help them both keep track of schedules. By being informative in this manner, she may calm the conversation.

## A Birthday Party Example

Sometimes the opposite occurs between parents. A parent may tell the other parent about an activity that exists for the children during the other parent's parenting time. Yet the other parent may resent being told what to do with his time, such as following:

> **(Katie)** Ben: Alison has a birthday party at Ella's house on Saturday at 10am during your time. She needs to be there on time with a present, and you should buy her an outfit from Nordstrom. Alison has something in mind for herself and wants to go to Nordstrom. Make sure she wears her new jeans and that she eats breakfast before she goes and eats all that cake.

**(Ben)** You can't tell me what to do during my parenting time. I have plans with the kids on Saturday and I'm not running all over town and wasting half the day in the car. You can't tell me what to feed my kids or how they dress anymore. I'm in charge. Mind your own business

What's a parent to do? *Telling* information might be taken wrong. *Not telling* information might also make someone mad and the children might miss out on activities or other important things.

Here's a possible BIFF response for Katie to Ben's angry response:

**(Katie)** I want to keep you informed when the children have a function or activity that I am aware of. I will make sure any possible activities are on the shared online calendar, and I will forward any email invitations they receive that fall on your time so you can make decisions and respond. I respect your right to make decisions about your time with the children.

That's it! That's all she needed to write. This looks like a BIFF response. What she left out is important. She didn't apologize for initially telling him what to do and what the child should wear, and she didn't respond to his "mind your own business" attack. She talked to him as an equal and, in her own words, acknowledged that he is an equal partner in parenting (making his own decisions). He also has equal responsibility to take care of social niceties such as responding to invitations.

She didn't try to hammer home to Ben that if he doesn't

let the children do their preferred activities during his time, the children are going to react in some way. Ben will figure that out on his own, and if she attempts to tell him how their children will react, he will see this as Katie telling him she's more in tune with their children than Ben is.

Most importantly, she didn't give him advice, at least not directly. She did mention that he would have to respond to invitations on his own.

Here's why she included what she did:

**Brief:** One paragraph is generally safe to get the point across without getting into triggering issues.

**Informative:** Katie backed off on telling Ben what to do, while gently pointing out that he has responsibilities regarding the children.

**Friendly:** She didn't make any direct friendly overtures here, but her tone is businesslike. She said she respected his right to make decisions about what the children do during his parenting time.

**Firm:** She states what she *will* do regarding the children's future activities. She clearly stated that he has some responsibilities as well as rights to the children.

## An Exchange and Rescheduling Example

John and Jericka's divorce was finished six months ago, but they still have frequent problems talking about routine parenting issues. Some Parenting Plans—whether court-ordered or developed by agreement—just aren't very detailed and have items missing that would help parents.

Even the most well-written Parenting Plan sometimes needs changes and flexibility. As mentioned earlier in this chapter, it can also be hard for a parent to realize that he or she simply isn't in charge during the other parent's time anymore, and the parents have differing opinions about what is most important for a child.

This communication example is pretty common with newly-divorced or separated parents. Practice a BIFF response for John to send to Jericka after the email exchange below:

**(John)** I'd like to have Christopher on Tuesday the 14th to attend a father-son baseball game at work. Tuesday is your night, but this is a special occasion, and I can trade you a night.

**(Jericka)** You have no respect at all for Christopher's homework or his need for a good night's sleep on school nights! You have no problem keeping him out late, doing nothing on homework, and then you leave me to deal with the consequences. You shouldn't be entitled to any school nights with him unless you're willing to do homework with him. You need to sign his reading list and spend at least two hours every night, and no, he can't play baseball on a school night!!!

[Note: Jericka never responded to the request to trade a night; she just changed the subject. This is common with people preoccupied with blaming others, who have trouble letting the other person control what's being discussed. And some Blamespeakers simply get so caught up in their anger that they are distracted from what was really being discussed.]

## Practice Exercise

If you want, try writing your own BIFF response for John, and check to see if it's Brief, Informative, Friendly and Firm. Also, see if it includes any admonishments, advice, or apologies. You can also practice at www.ConflictPlaybook.com.

# BIFF for CoParent Communication

**Brief?**
☐ Yes
☐ No
☐ Maybe

**Informative?**
☐ Yes
☐ No
☐ Maybe

**Friendly?**
☐ Yes
☐ No
☐ Maybe

**Firm?**
☐ Yes
☐ No
☐ Maybe

**Advice?**
☐ Yes
☐ No
☐ Maybe

**Admonishments?**
☐ Yes
☐ No
☐ Maybe

**Apologies?**
☐ Yes
☐ No
☐ Maybe

## Sample Response

Here's one way of writing a response for John, but remember, there is no one absolutely correct response. Every BIFF needs to fit the reader, the writer and the unique current situation. So, yours might be similar or different. Just try to keep it Brief, Informative, Friendly and Firm. See what you think of this one:

**(John)**

Hi Carol:

Thanks for responding to my request right away.

I understand your concern about Christopher's homework, and I share that concern. I can have him work on his homework immediately after school is out, so that he has it done before the game on Tuesday the 14th. We will also do any studying that can be done ahead of time when I have him the weekend before this game.

I am open to switching days with you when there are special mother-son events. This type of flexibility will make us both look good and will show Christopher that we can cooperate for his benefit. Now that we've discussed how his homework will be done on Tuesday the 14th to allow him this game, I will plan to pick him up from school on Tuesday the 14th, and I would like to exchange a date for you right away. Please confirm the date you would like in exchange.

John

As mentioned above, one problem with frequent Blamespeakers is that sometimes they can't answer a simple, straightforward question with a straightforward answer. They often ignore other people's questions and raise new issues of their own, and the new issues are often addressed in an attacking manner. It's hard, but important, to stay focused and not slip into reacting to the Blamespeaker's distracting comments. Stick to the issue at hand. Going off on the distraction that the Blamespeaker has raised with you won't lead to effective communications.

Notice how John handled this problem by focusing back onto his request to exchange a day with Jericka, and he didn't get hooked by her distraction about homework. He also didn't respond to or get mad about her demands that he do certain things about the homework. He connected with her *concern* about homework, validated her concern, and then brought the discussion back to his initial request. He was informative about the attention he would give the homework so Jericka could hear that he had made her concern an important issue.

Also note that John took a risk by planning to just show up at school to pick up the child on Tuesday, in violation of Jericka's original statement "no baseball". But John presented this as new information which should lead to a new solution rather than the angry confrontation that Jericka attempted. And, he still left the door open for her to say "no" again. He pushed back but is letting her know he feels strongly about this issue. If Jericka responds angrily and off-topic again, he can choose to continue to respond to her in the same way or back off.

## Choosing Your Battles

It often helps to think in terms of choosing your battles when thinking about BIFF communications. With frequent Blamespeakers (also known as high conflict people or HCPs), there is so much that they may bombard their coparent with, that you have to pick and choose what to ignore and what to fight for.

With this in mind, some people faced with a statement like Jericka's about the homework might completely ignore that distraction and not even mention it. They may be used to having their *Jericka* ignore requests and respond with demands. They also may be used to her forgetting about what she said, so that not mentioning it may be better so that it doesn't bring her attention back to her homework comment.

Other parents may find that they need to respond in depth to the homework statement, because they know that this is a top issue for their *Jericka*. This is an example of weighing your knowledge of your coparent in choosing how to respond with your BIFF.

## Evidence for Court

There's another consideration when writing your BIFF communication. What if your conversation shows up in court someday because the other person submits it or you decide it's in your interests to submit what each of you said on an issue? In this case, by fully explaining himself and staying on the subject of his request for a trade, John can show a family law judge these emails as evidence at court someday, if necessary. Jericka's refusal and angry, off-topic responses, will likely show her in a bad light, and John has made a strong case for his own reasonableness and responsiveness in writing. He made a reasonable request, responded to her concerns, and made it clear that he would do the same for her in the future. Judges like to see respectful communication between coparents.

If Jericka, or any Blamespeaker, keeps responding and trying to keep the conflict going, the other person can ultimately say: "I've said all I'm going to say on this subject. Have a good weekend." Or they could say something similar. That person then can stop responding altogether.

# Conclusion

The BIFF examples in this chapter can be used with your coparent. The relationship you have with a coparent is an unavoidable one: you have a child together. Generally, this is a relationship you don't have the ability to end completely. Sometimes the coparent is so toxic to you that if you didn't have a child together, under no circumstances would you continue any relationship with this person. A friendship or romantic relationship would have been terminated long ago. But because you share a child, you are forced to find some way to make this relationship work in order to raise your child.

The examples are not absolute rules about how you can respond to a variety of difficult situations with a Blamespeaker coparent using BIFF communications. BIFFs require a balanced approach, not mean or confrontational. BIFF will help you set limits and focus on solving problems rather than just reacting and lashing out.

**A caution is important here:** sometimes a Blamespeaker sets up communications in a way to goad you into reacting, and by reacting may make you (the responder) look like the problem in the communication. No matter how you are baited, it's important to check yourself to ensure you are responding rather than reacting. Don't allow yourself to fall into the trap of becoming abusive or accusatory in response. **Picture your responses being read by a judge in a courtroom.** You want to be the parent who *always* uses BIFF communications.

The two most important principles to remember at all times when communicating with a Blamespeaker are:

**1. Stay focused.** The person you're communicating with has great difficulty letting others take the initiative in conversations and doesn't like it when you set limits with them. You have full responsibility for focusing on the issue at hand and returning communications back to that issue, no matter what. A high conflict coparent may completely ignore your requests, change the subject, and raise extreme demands of their own, often by counter-attacking.

**2. Don't react!** Reacting to the high conflict communication is distraction, which is exactly what the Blamespeaker wants. By focusing on your goals and on a BIFF response, you can contain the situation and not let it get out of hand.

# CHAPTER FIVE

# BIFFs About Education

Parents have an awesome responsibility to educate their children and to prepare them to successfully face the adult world in only 18 years. This responsibility is the source of a lot of joy and celebration and also can be the source of much conflict between parents who are not cooperating well with one another.

There are many ways that parent's help their children learn and develop. It starts at birth as we engage our babies, holding, talking, bathing, soothing, and so much more. Our effort to help them develop into happy, healthy, effective people continues for the rest of our lives. And much of the work of helping our children develop we do ourselves. But we also engage our children in the lives of our communities, eliciting the help of others. Childcare providers, coaches, teachers, and informal mentors are just a few of the kinds of people who help guide the development of our children.

Parents face many choices, many problems to be solved, in arranging for providers, coaches, school, and the myriad other adults who will provide formal and informal education. Using the BIFF method of communication can improve success in agreeing on providers, and in maintaining their participation with your children.

# A Childcare Example

Will and Meg are facing the need for child care for their 8-month-old daughter, Ann, as Meg has taken a new job, and Will also has job responsibilities outside the home that will not allow him to care for Ann during the work day.

> **(Meg)** Will, I will be returning to work beginning in three weeks. I will need childcare for Ann from 7:15 am to 5:45 pm each day, Monday to Friday. I suggest that we jointly put her in a licensed, professionally operated, childcare facility that is located within a 15-minute drive of both of our homes. While I would love to have her attend the very finest childcare in the metropolitan area that would feed into a preschool that prepares children for a college bound education, I don't have the money right now to pay those kinds of prices. I am still having to pay for attorneys and counselors because you won't coparent with me. So, because you are spending all of our money on this court stuff, our daughter will have to go somewhere not as good. So, I suggest Happy Children Daycare. And you have not yet gotten me paid the money you owe for medical expenses from the last four months. I suggest you get with your attorney and have her tell you what is going to happen to you if you don't get me paid. It is very hard to find daycare providers for children Ann's age. Happy Children Daycare has an opening right now, so I must have your agreement by the end of the day tomorrow if we are going to work together on this.

So, let's take a look. How did Meg do at writing an effect BIFF message?

# BIFF CHECKER

**Brief?** (Usually 2-5 sentences)

☐ Yes
☐ No
☑ Maybe

On this criterion she could use some improvement. Eleven sentences are more than twice as long as it needs to be and the message certainly loses focus.

**Informative?** (Who, what, when, where, what for?)

☐ Yes
☐ No
☑ Maybe

Meg starts out strong. She identifies the challenge—she is returning to work in three weeks. She clearly states her need for childcare and for a specific period of time on specific days. She makes a statement about what is informing her decision making. And she does make a clear proposal about which childcare she wants to use, but she fails to identify the cost of the service or the location of the childcare.

**Friendly?**

☐ Yes
☑ No
☐ Maybe

Not very. She does use Will's name but there is no greeting at the beginning and no salutation at the end. Meg just drops into the proposal and ends it with a pretty strong demand.

**Firm?**

☑ Yes
☐ No
☐ Maybe

It is certainly firm. Meg offers one proposal with very a tight time frame.

**Advice?**

☑ Yes
☐ No
☐ Maybe

Meg seems to have gotten a bit off course when she started to make the suggestion about which facility to use. She advises Will to get with his attorney.

**Admonishments?**

☑ Yes
☐ No
☐ Maybe

Meg is frustrated about things that are not directly tied to the proposal she is making but uses this message as an opportunity to bring them up when she criticizes Will for not yet getting her paid for past expenses.

**Apologies?**
☐ Yes
☑ No
☐ Maybe

To her credit, Meg does not apologize in this communication.

And so, Will prepares to respond to the message. Will has been taking seriously the idea of trying to work well with Meg, and so has requested and received some coaching. The first thing he does is check his emotional response to see if he has become defensive in response to the message. And yes, he does feel somewhat pushed by the message.

**Editing the message he received:** A suggestion that he has found particularly helpful is to take a little time to *edit a message that comes to him* before he begins to put together a reply. That way he can figure out if there is a real problem for him to respond to. Often there is—it's just hidden in the insults and demands. Sometimes, it's just venting and there's nothing that needs a response.

In this case, he identifies that the problem that they are trying to solve is providing childcare for Ann. So he edits the message to stay focused on that one concern, putting aside the insults and demands. After a bit of editing Meg's message, this is what it looks like and what Will is going to respond to:

**Will's attempt at editing Meg's email:**

Will, I will be returning to work beginning in three weeks. I will need childcare for Ann from 7:15 am to 5:45 pm each day, Monday to Friday. I suggest that we jointly put her in a licensed, professionally operated, childcare facility that is located within a 15-minute drive of both of our homes. I suggest Happy Children Daycare. It is very hard to find daycare providers for children Ann's age. Happy Children Daycare has an opening right now, so I [need to know your answer] by the end of the day tomorrow.

Will takes a few moments to look at the daycare's website, calls the facility to ask a few questions and puts together his reply.

First, he allows himself to write a very nasty sentence, then he throws it away and writes the following.

Meg,

I am so glad that you got the job, Congratulations.

I like your standards of a licensed, professionally operated childcare facility that is relatively close to both our homes. Happy Children Daycare has many good reviews online, so I am inclined toward it as well. I want to actually see the place where Ann would be each day, so I have arranged to visit the facility day after tomorrow. The cost will be $240 per week, which I would be willing to pay 50%. I suggest that we would each pay the Daycare directly. I am prepared to agree to using this daycare and will contact you with my actual decision as soon as I finish the facility visit in two days.

I hope you are doing well.

Will

How did Will do?

# BIFF CHECKER

**Brief?** (Usually 2-5 sentences)

It contains six sentences, but Will stays focused on the problem being solved.

**Informative?** (Who, what, when, where, what for?)

It indicates that Will is thinking about the daycare, what he needs to do to provide a final decision and when that decision will be made and communicated to Meg. It also makes a clear proposal about the issue that was left out of the communication from Meg.

**Friendly?**

Both at the beginning and at the end. Will also maintains a positive tone throughout the message.

**Firm?**

☑ Yes
☐ No
☐ Maybe

Will offered clear information, an indication of his answer, and a firm date/time for his final decision.

**Advice?**

☐ Yes
☑ No
☐ Maybe

**Admonishments?**

☐ Yes
☑ No
☐ Maybe

**Apologies?**

☐ Yes
☑ No
☐ Maybe

## When Educators are Brought into the Fray

Often high conflict parents think that they are helping a situation when they involve teachers, coaches, or other educators in the discussions between the parents. They copy the educators on emails or include them in text threads. At times they even bring the conflict directly to the educator, which can put educators in very difficult situation if left unaddressed, especially when one parent leaves the other parent out of the communication with the teacher.

## A School Teacher Example

Dan wrote to his daughter Alice's second grade teacher, copying Lucy (Alice's mother):

**(Dan)**

Ms. Johanson,

I am very upset about the way you are refusing to communicate with me. As I am sure you know, Alice's mother and I are in the midst of a nasty divorce. Alice's mother is slandering me and has falsely accused me of abusing Alice and her younger brother. She has tried to cut me out of being their father and is trying to stop my participation in their lives entirely. I will not let this happen. I would have thought you as a professional teacher would have known better than to cut me out and I demand that you send me all information that you send to Alice's mother. Further, I expect to be invited to all meetings that Alice's mother is invited to.

I expect you to respond immediately,

Dan

Lucy was upset by Dan's email and quickly began to put together a reply.

**Lucy's** First Draft Email (not sent):

Dan,

What are you doing? You know better than to drag our divorce into our daughter's school. Ms. Johanson has nothing to do with the school's email system and who gets one email or another. You are blowing this all out of proportion, but I guess that is no surprise, you have a long history of losing your temper and saying things that hurt our daughter...

But, Lucy had recently been to a class on reducing conflict between parents and realized that her initial response to the email was only going to escalate the conflict between them. Still she knew that Ms. Johanson was likely to respond herself and did not want to miss the opportunity to take Ms. Johanson out of the conflict if possible.

So, she wrote:

**Lucy's Email (sent):**

Ms. Johanson, and Dan,

As Alice's parents we have always been very committed to Alice's education and supportive of the fine work that the school district and you have done to help her learn. Further, I have always been impressed with the districts efforts to keep parents informed about what is going on at the school and how our children are doing.

Let me see if I can address Dan's concerns. I believe that there may have been some confusion about a conversation that Ms. Johanson and I had in passing at the grocery store last week.

Ms. Johanson and I happened to run into one another at the market on the weekend and stopped to chat for just a few minutes. I then shared with you, Dan, what Ms. Johanson and I talked about. I understand how you could think that Ms. Johanson had come to me with concerns without including you. That was not the case. Dan, going forward I will be clear about how information is shared with me.

I hope this addresses this concern.

Sincerely,

Lucy

So, how did Lucy do?

# BIFF CHECKER

**Brief?** (Usually 2-5 sentences)

Lucy did not stay within the 2-5 sentences guideline, but this situation called for bit more. Let's see how she did with the other elements to see if the length is really a problem.

**Informative?** (Who, what, when, where, what for?)

Lucy provided the information needed to explain the situation, and clarified what had happened.

**Friendly?**

☑ Yes
☐ No
☐ Maybe

Lucy begins by offering affirmation of both the teacher and the school district. She also offers understanding of how Dan might have gotten upset. She does not blame Dan and does not get caught up in an agreement about the divorce.

**Firm?**

☑ Yes
☐ No
☐ Maybe

Lucy takes control of the conversation and stays focused on the current problem and offers a solution that she can be responsible for.

**Advice?**

**Admonishments?**
☐ Yes
☑ No
☐ Maybe

Certainly Lucy could have gotten distracted by criticizing Dan for the way he approached Ms. Johanson, but instead stays focused on resolving the issue and not furthering the conflict.

**Apologies?**
☐ Yes
☑ No
☐ Maybe

Lucy takes responsibility for the miscommunication and commits herself to different behavior in the future; however, she does not apologize directly.

**A Suggestion**

Overall, Lucy's email may feel a little long, which risks triggering Dan's defensiveness. Therefore, one suggestion would be to take out the middle paragraph. If you were in Lucy's shoes, you could read her email out loud with the paragraph and then without that paragraph. Then decide which way sounded better. Try it yourself and see what you think. Remember, there's no one right way to write a BIFF communication, so long as it is Brief, Informative, Friendly and Firm.

## Writing to Both

This is a case in which Lucy needed to decide who to respond to, if she responded at all. It certainly seems like a situation that begs a response before things get out of hand with the teacher. In at least one situation we are aware of, a school told parents that they could not keep their child in the school because of the way the parents' conflicts were impacting other children, other parents and the school. So, she needs to respond.

While she started out writing to Dan, she realized she needed to write to the teacher as well, as soon as possible. Deciding to write to both in the same email appears to be an excellent way to deal with this: she helps the teacher understand what's going on, she helps Dan know what really happened with the teacher, and she includes them together so there are no secrets or fears of secrets.

As suggested in Chapter 2, it often helps to respond to everyone who was included in the initial difficult communication, so that everyone gets the same information so that any misinformation is cleared up as soon as possible before it settles in.

# Conclusion

In short, it is always important to stay focused on the problem we are trying to solve. In the first example in this chapter, Will helped himself focus by editing out all the unnecessary comments in the message he received so that he would only address what was necessary. This helped him avoid accidently over-reacting to the many emotional statements it contained if he kept looking at them in preparing his BIFF response.

In the second example, Lucy focused on jointly communicating with Dan and the teacher, which informed them both while also showing that she wasn't having any secret communication with either one.

If we get distracted and bring in other concerns or frustrations, we can open up the opportunity for Blamespeakers to get defensive. Once that happens, the opportunity to cooperate disappears quickly, or at least becomes very difficult. We certainly don't want that to happen in the midst of working with those we have enlisted in helping us educate our children.

# CHAPTER SIX

# BIFFs about Healthcare

In some cases where parents fail to communicate, the loss to the child is a missed activity or being late to school. But in cases involving healthcare, the parents' failure to communicate effectively could result in physical harm or pain to a child.

Parents obviously are very concerned with their child's health and healthcare. Fears about a child's health can combine with negative feelings about the other parent to result in even higher levels of blame and accusation.

## An Illness Example

Imagine this communication:

### (Carlos Email to Maria)

When I got Junior today, he had an ear infection and needed to be taken to the doctor. The doctor said it was obvious that he got sick at your house over the weekend and YOU DID NOTHING ABOUT IT! He prescribed antibiotics which you will need to make sure he takes twice a day in his ear. I am sending the bottle with him to school tomorrow so make sure he has it in his backpack when you pick him up. Once again you have been IRRESPONSIBLE about Junior's healthcare and I have to clean up after your irresponsibility. I will discuss this with my lawyer and decide whether to return to court to reduce your parenting time for the health and safety of our son!

Carlos isn't communicating effectively with Maria, but Carlos is also frightened and angry as he feels their child suffered needlessly.

### Practice Exercise

**Your turn to practice. Write a BIFF response to this email as Maria.** Assume the following background information: Junior had no signs of an ear infection on the weekend, and you know those signs can come on quickly. Also, Maria remembers that Carlos once took Junior on a camping trip when he got a leg fracture and didn't seek treatment because he thought it was just a bruise. That time, Maria took Junior to the doctor and an x-ray showed he had a hairline fracture.

Remember to check your response to see if it's Brief, Informative, Friendly and Firm. Also, see if it includes any admonishments, advice, or apologies. You can also practice at www.ConflictPlaybook.com.

_____

_____

_____

_____

_____

_____

_____

_____

_____

_____

_____

Take a notepad and make your own BIFF Checker. Is your message BIFF?

## Sample BIFF Response

**Maria's Draft Email to Carlos (didn't send)**

Thank you for taking Junior to the doctor. (Friendly) I will follow the directions for his medication. I was not irresponsible with Junior and he had no signs of an ear infection while with me. As you may know, those symptoms can come on very quickly. (Informative) I am fairly sure the doctor did not tell you that he obviously got this ear infection while with me. (Firm) I will keep you advised of Junior's condition while he is with me.

So, how did Maria do?

# BIFF CHECKER

---

**Brief?** (Usually 2-5 sentences)

☑ Yes
☐ No
☐ Maybe

Fairly brief, just six sentences—a reasonable paragraph.

---

**Informative?** (Who, what, when, where, what for?)

☑ Yes
☐ No
☐ Maybe

Maria provided the information that there were no signs of an infection over the weekend and that symptoms can appear suddenly. However, she also had some defensiveness ("I was not irresponsible...") that doesn't seem necessary. The sentence about the doctor also appears unnecessary, perhaps a little sarcastic ("obviously got" it with me).

---

**Friendly?**

☐ Yes
☐ No
☑ Maybe

The phrase and sentence mentioned above make it less friendly without adding any benefit.

**Firm?**
- ☐ Yes
- ☐ No
- ☑ Maybe

The comment about the doctor may trigger an unnecessary defensive response from Carlos.

**Advice?**
- ☐ Yes
- ☑ No
- ☐ Maybe

**Admonishments?**
- ☐ Yes
- ☐ No
- ☑ Maybe

The comment about the doctor might feel like she's admonishing him by bringing the unlikely comments of the doctor into the discussion.

**Apologies?**
- ☐ Yes
- ☑ No
- ☐ Maybe

**A suggestion:** Maria could read this out loud without the phrase about irresponsibility and the sentence about the doctor to hear how it sounds. This is how it would read. What do you think?

Carlos—thank you for taking Junior to the doctor. I will follow the directions for his medication. Junior had no signs of an ear infection while with me. As you may know, those symptoms can come on very quickly. I will keep you advised of Junior's condition while he is with me.

## A Final Note About Omitting the Leg Incident

Maria chose not to bring up the past incident involving the leg fracture. While that was concerning to her at the time, it has little or nothing to do with Carlos' current accusations or Junior's present health. Including that would just escalate the situation. However, if Carlos complained about the ear infection someday in court papers or a hearing, then it would be appropriate to explain the fractured leg incident to put things in proper perspective. But just between the coparents, this isn't necessary to bring up.

# A Medical Appointment Example

### Including a Medical Provider in Parents' Emails

When children are getting medical or psychological care, appointments with providers are really important. A failure to show up on time can result in late fees or the cancellation of the appointment. When an appointment is about something anxiety-producing, like parent-child counseling, or testing for something that might be serious, emotions are high. If one parent perceives that the other parent isn't taking the appointments seriously, communications can get out of hand, and BIFF communications become more important than ever.

> **From: Carlos**
>
> **To: Maria and Kristi's counselor, Dr. Gastin**
>
> Kristi arrived to our mutual, father-daughter counseling session 30 minutes late tonight and also late last Tuesday, November 12. Both times Kristi arrived after Dr. Gastin's office texted Maria to remind her that there was an appointment scheduled.
>
> I am only able to be with Kristi for one hour per week so it is extremely disappointing when I am not able to spend a full hour with her. This is the only time we have to work on issues that will allow us more time in the future. I would ask that time and resources committed by Dr. Gastin and I be respected going forward.

Carlos did a good job at keeping this communication in BIFF form, by being fairly brief, very informative (he has stated facts as he understands them), fairly friendly, and firm about asking that the appointment times be respected in the future.

This email was a bit different, as Kristi's counselor, Dr. Gastin, was included in the email. The counselor may or may not want to be a part of the parents' communications. Because the issue directly involved Kristi's counseling, it's likely okay that Carlos included Dr. Gastin in the email, so the doctor is aware that lateness is an issue that Carlos really wants addressed. Most children's counselors will be familiar with coparenting communication difficulties that directly affect the child's counseling sessions.

Be cautious, however, about including medical and similar providers in the emails. Unless the issue directly involves the child's appointments, as it did in this example, the providers more than likely do not want to be involved in the parents' emails unless specific information about the child is involved.

# An Advance Notice Example

## Notification of Appointments

Sometimes notification of a child's appointments is forgotten, which results not only in miscommunication but delays in getting the child treatment.

> **From: Maria**
>
> **To: Carlos**
>
> **Re: Kristi dentist**
>
> Kristi went to the dentist last week and he says she needs two fillings and should be evaluated for braces soon. You owe me your share for this appointment. While she is only 9, she may need braces early. They will cost about $2000 and your portion will be $1500. She will be having the fillings done and the evaluation in the next few weeks.

Unfortunately, this email was Carlos' first notification of anything going on at the dentist. He responded.

**From: Carlos**

**To: Maria**

**Re: re Kristi dentist**

HOW DARE YOU take her to the dentist without telling me? Who did you even take her to? Why was I not told of her appointment and given the chance to go? I WON'T PAY FOR ANYTHING and I'm taking you to court for ignoring my rights to be at her dentist appointment. You did this two years ago when she was taken in for vaccinations without telling me and YOU SHOULD KNOW BETTER.

What was wrong with Maria's original email about the dentist? While she could argue it was somewhat informative (she provided information mostly about money), a lot of information that a coparent should have is missing from her email. She didn't tell Carlos about the appointment in advance and she doesn't give him the name of the dentist. It sounds like Maria may have chosen the dentist on her own without consulting Carlos, which does not follow the requirements of most parenting agreements that include "Joint" legal custody regarding big decisions like healthcare and education. And, Maria simply tells Carlos that the future dental work will be scheduled, without asking for his input and without telling him the date of the future appointment.

Carlos' response is angry and threatening, and ignores any discussion of the child's healthcare. He (probably correctly) points out things Maria has done wrong, but his objections to Maria's actions are lost in his angry email.

Carlos—I did forget to tell you the dentist's name. It is Dr. Nelson at Pediatric Dental Care on Morton Road. The appointment was made so long ago and I thought I had told you about it, but I obviously forgot. I understand that you will want to talk with Dr. Nelson about what he suggests for Kristi. As I always handled the appointments for the children while we were together, I thought that I should keep doing that, but it won't happen again.

Note that Maria quickly acknowledged her failure to give the dentist's name, but she did not apologize. She gave a brief *excuse* for making the appointment without Carlos and mentioned past events ("I always handled the appointments"), which probably isn't necessary, but she did not apologize and simply said "it won't happen again." This keeps the focus on the future and what to do in the future, rather than focusing Carlos' attention on her mistake.

On the other hand, if Carlos wanted to change the tone of their emails and communicate in a BIFF manner, he could have responded to Maria's original email like this:

### Carlos BIFF Email to Maria

I was surprised to hear of the dentist appointment as I didn't know about it. Before making appointments, please send me the name of the doctor and the date and time, so I can participate. First, please send me the name of the dentist she saw, and I will talk to that person directly and get the information I need. You are not authorized to make any more appointments with this dentist or another healthcare professional until I have had the chance to get information. Please see Section 8 of our parenting agreement that requires that we act jointly for healthcare decisions.

Carlos' alternative email is a BIFF. It's informative, as he references that he should have had notice, and he now needs the doctor's name. It is friendly and firm. He kept it brief by not bringing up past offenses which may not be relevant to the issue of her current dental care, but he is firm that he has read their parenting agreement and insists that it be followed. That should end the conversation in a constructive manner. Of course, some might say that the last sentence is an admonishment, but others might say it is appropriate. It is always a judgment call and up to the BIFF writer. In this case, it seems appropriate to us that it be included.

## An Information Exchange Example

### Exchange of information about providers and locations:

From: Julie

To: Lonnie

Lonnie, Jayden's doctor appointment is scheduled with Dr. Smith on Tuesday. I'm notifying you as required by our parenting plan, even though you've never taken the kids to a doctor appointment in your life.

This email is brief, but not much else. It's not informative, as there are likely numerous Dr. Smith's in most localities, and no address or contact information is given. It simply says it's a doctor appointment, without stating whether anything is wrong with Jayden. The email is definitely not friendly, considering the denigrating last phrase. And, it's possible that the doctor's name was intentionally left vague, to try and make Lonnie embarrass himself by admitting that he doesn't know his child's doctor's name.

An appropriate BIFF communication about a doctor's appointment could be:

> Lonnie, Jayden's well-check doctor appointment, to include a flu shot, is scheduled with Dr. Raymond Smith, Choice Pediatrics (Gilbert Road), on Tuesday 9-5 at 10:30am.
>
> Julie

That's all that's needed for appropriate notification. Even if a parent is quite sure that the other parent knows who Dr. Smith is, or where Dr. Smith's office is located, including all the information is more respectful to both parents. While this still may feel too brief, it depends on the situation between the parents. In some cases, an additional friendly comment could be made. In other cases, just the facts may be sufficient and both parents may agree that this is the way to do it without risking triggering anything else.

## A Healthcare Provider Example

Communications with healthcare providers (doctors, dentists, therapists, and others) also need to be BIFF, with an emphasis on the Brief and Informative parts. As mentioned about Dr. Gastin and the late arrivals in Carlos and Maria's example above, healthcare providers (including therapists) do not have the time to read long, angry emails between parents. They also generally don't need or want to read about past transgressions between the parents. The provider's concern is with their role in the child's medical care, and parents should be cautious to stick to direct information about the child that the provider needs to know.

### Mother's Email to Father, Copied to Child's Pediatrician:

Well, you've done it again. You must have fed Danielle strawberries, because she woke up with hives and a sore throat. I had to immediately give her Benadryl and sit up with her for hours. You've known since she was 3 years old that she has this reaction to strawberries, but I'm sure you're too busy with your girlfriend and the new house to pay attention to what your daughter is eating. The next time, I'm driving her straight to the emergency room and sticking you with the bill, and I'm sure Dr. Raymond would agree!

First, did Dr. Raymond need to be copied on this email at all? It doesn't appear so, because presumably if the child needed a doctor, Mother would have called him already. The email is not BIFF, as it's not brief and offers little information. Mother made a conclusion that strawberries were the culprit, without any apparent evidence, and seeks mainly to insult Father's parenting in the email, possibly with the hope that Dr. Raymond will have a negative view of Father. While Dr. Raymond undoubtedly needs to know at some point that the child had a reaction to something, emails like this are not the answer.

If a child's provider does want to receive emails about incidents like this, what could a BIFF communication look like? Try re-writing Mothers' email, then see an example below. Remember to check your response to see if it's Brief, Informative, Friendly and Firm. Also, see if it includes any admonishments, advice, or apologies. You can also practice at www.ConflictPlaybook.com.

_____

_____

_____

_____

_____

_____

_____

_____

_____

_____

_____

**Mother's Email to Father, Copied to Child's Pediatrician:**

Danielle came home to my house (from you) about 8pm, and by midnight she had woken up with hives and complained of a sore throat. I gave her Benadryl and we were up for hours. She seems to have had a reaction to something while at your house. Would you give Dr. Raymond and me information, as soon as possible, about what she ate and did while at your home so we can try to get to the bottom of this?

So, how did Mother do?

# BIFF CHECKER

---

**Brief?** (Usually 2-5 sentences)

Brief and to the point. Just four sentences—a reasonable paragraph.

---

**Informative?** (Who, what, when, where, what for?)

It simply informs Father and Dr. Raymond about what happened, without assuming as-yet unknown facts (about strawberries).

**Friendly?**   ☐ Yes
                ☐ No
                ☑ Maybe

Minimally, but probably sufficient. She approaches it as a team of all three of them: "so we can try to get to the bottom of this."

**Firm?**   ☑ Yes
            ☐ No
            ☐ Maybe

She asks for him to respond "as soon as possible."

**Advice?**   ☐ Yes
              ☑ No
              ☐ Maybe

**Admonishments?**   ☐ Yes
                    ☑ No
                    ☐ Maybe

Unlike the prior example of hers.

**Apologies?**   ☐ Yes
                 ☑ No
                 ☐ Maybe

If Dr. Raymond has in fact asked to receive emails like this, he can form an opinion that this parent is interested in finding out what happened to the child, and not just insulting the other parent.

# A Special Diet Example

## Specialists and Particular Medical Issues

Most of the examples given so far have been about fairly routine medical communications like appointments, flu shots, well child visits, and hives. Unfortunately, some co-parents have to discuss far more serious medical issues.

As background to this sample email, Angelina and Frank are the parents of Ben, who is now four. Ben has had developmental and physical issues almost since birth. He has a special diet and has several occupational and physical therapies on a regular basis. While Frank had limited parenting time with Ben for the first year of his life, Frank has had close to equal parenting time for the last three years, and the parents attend almost all doctor and specialist appointments together. Recently, Angelina sent Frank this email:

**From: Angelina**

**To: Frank**

**Re: Ben**

LATE

You were 15 minutes late again today and Monday you were half an hour late because you decided to go to Pure Sushi instead of dropping off Ben on time when you knew I was waiting. You just do whatever you want and it's not helping.

DIET

When Ben came home today, he had diarrhea. He had chicken nuggets today? That alone might do it, but what other foods did he have that we might need to eliminate?

Again, he needs to be on a vegetarian diet for his syndrome. High on fresh fruit and veggies. Why do you keep giving him meat?

You met with his pediatrician with your concerns about him being on a vegetarian diet and she also explained to you that it was safe and beneficial. You also asked his caretaker about the same thing and they explained it was beneficial. What will it take to convince you?

Ben is blood type O positive, like me, and that blood type benefits greatly from this diet. Below is part of an article from the medical journal about his syndrome.

[Two-page long excerpt from medical journal inserted]

This isn't a fad diet. It could be a matter of life or death for him.

I know you're not adhering, because he comes back to me with hives and stomach pain. He should also be drinking about 56 oz a day now for his size/age to stay hydrated. His recommended diet is:

(2) 8oz cups of oat milk in the morning
8oz of "juice" ("juice" for us means 25%juice mixed with 75% water) at lunch

8oz of "juice"/water before nap
8oz of "juice"/water after nap
8oz of "juice"/water with dinner
8oz oat milk during reading time before bed.

Add more liquids if he's in the heat as dehydration is a concern. Nutrients that are thicker like healthy berry juices are absorbed better—just make sure he has water too.

He came home with a cracked lip today too. His skin is delicate. Please make sure he's hydrated.

I have read tons of information on his syndrome over the years and how to best treat to have a normal life. Diet alone can eliminate many symptoms. And starting now will save him from having many issues as he gets older. It's just second nature to me now, but you need to follow.

A vegetarian diet works best for us and we occasionally eat fish on Sundays (salmon, cod or mackerel). Ben doesn't like salmon much but will have a bite of cod every now and then in fish tacos or mackerel tossed in veggie pastas. We are not totally gluten free but we do feel better with other grains, like spelt, black bean, rice flour, lentil flour pastas. We make pizzas out of Indian or Mediterranean flatbread instead of regular dough and pesto with fresh mozzarella. But he usually eats chopped cooked and fresh veggies and fruit.

We avoid nightshades (tomatoes, potatoes, peppers, eggplants). His blood type is typically sensitive—they cause heartburn and inflammation so Ben and I just avoid them too even if we are not technically "allergic." Follow the Eat Right for your type blood type app on your phone for green type A foods that are beneficial to him and avoid the ones in red.

ALLERGIES
To help with Ben's allergies and sensitive skin, please use scent free/dye free soaps and detergents, latex free bandages, no harsh adhesives which can tear the skin.

Whew! That's a lot to take in. Angelina seems to feel that Frank needs a lot of education about their son's needs. This communication isn't BIFF in any way. How could Angelina have possibly given all this information in a brief format? She probably couldn't, but based on the background of their case, it doesn't seem all this information was necessary from Angelina. She knows that Frank consults with the doctor and is present at most appointments, and that about half of Ben's therapies take place during Frank's parenting time. So, *brief* in this case could have been accomplished by Angelina saying "You meet with Ben's doctors, so you know his recommended diet and that he has to stay well hydrated."

This email isn't even *informative*, despite its length, because there is so much information that it isn't really useful. There's just too much, and this type of information should be coming from Ben's doctors. It's not *friendly:* It starts out with accusations of being late, and continues with accusations that Frank feeds Ben inappropriate things. The tone of the email speaks to Frank as if he's just meeting his son for the first time, instead of the actual history that Frank has been a big part of his life.

As Angelina apparently has some concerns about recent difficulties Ben is suffering, she can try to make her email more BIFF:

> **From: Angelina**
>
> **To: Frank**
>
> When Ben came home today, he had diarrhea which gives me some concerns about his diet. He also had a cracked lip. I know you are aware, from his doctor, about his dietary restrictions and that he needs to stay well-hydrated. Do you know of anything recently that has changed with his diet, that could have caused this problem?
>
> I read a lot about his syndrome, and if you would be agreeable, I'd like to have a discussion about his diet in each of our homes and what has worked for me. I would also be glad to share what soaps and hypo-allergenic products are used in my home, as his skin is so sensitive. Would you be agreeable to having a discussion about these things?

How did Angelina do this time?

## BIFF CHECKER

**Brief?** (Usually 2-5 sentences)

☐ Yes
☐ No
☑ Maybe

Fairly brief. In order to be BIFF, Angelina will have to realize that Ben's doctors are the main source of information about his medical needs, and while she and Frank should talk about those needs and how to coordinate care, she does not dictate what Frank feeds or does for Ben.

**Informative?** (Who, what, when, where, what for?)

☑ Yes
☐ No
☐ Maybe

Sufficiently for this purpose. Admittedly, if Frank did not have a background of significant involvement with Ben's medical providers, Angelina's emails would have to be more than brief, in order to give adequate information. But too much at once, as in her first example, negates all of it. That's the benefit of brief communications.

**Friendly?**

☐ Yes
☐ No
☑ Maybe

Minimally, but sufficient. She offers to share the knowledge she has gained, without being insulting about it. By asking, rather than telling, she is respectful of his right to say "Yes" or "No" to her offer.

**Firm?**

☑ Yes
☐ No
☐ Maybe

She sufficiently ends the conversation with her offer to provide information, to which he can say "Yes" or "No." Remember, firm means ending any hostilities in the conversation, not being harsh.

---

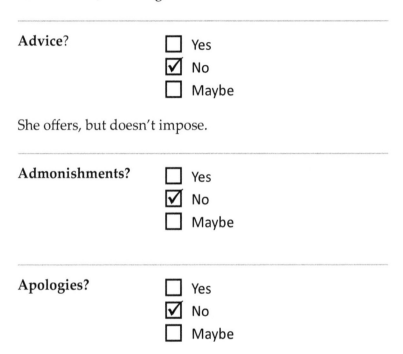

**Advice?**　　　　☐ Yes
　　　　　　　　　☑ No
　　　　　　　　　☐ Maybe

She offers, but doesn't impose.

---

**Admonishments?**　☐ Yes
　　　　　　　　　☑ No
　　　　　　　　　☐ Maybe

---

**Apologies?**　　　☐ Yes
　　　　　　　　　☑ No
　　　　　　　　　☐ Maybe

**Asking if he wants her information:** This is an important idea. If you have information that the other parent could or should use, its best to offer it, rather than impose it. Asking if your coparent wants some information is the best way to open the subject. If he or she says "No," then just drop it. You can only make it worse by insisting that they accept your information, which usually feels a lot like your advice, which you already know doesn't work.

With practice, even the most serious of a child's medical issues can be discussed in a BIFF format. Upon receiving

Angelina's first, extremely long email, Frank could respond with a BIFF like this, to put some boundaries around their communications:

> **From: Frank**
>
> **To: Angelina**
>
> Angelina, I received your long email about Ben's nutritional and other needs. As you know, I attend the majority of his doctor's appointments and consult with his doctors and therapists frequently. I have the same information you have about nutrition, including a primarily vegetarian diet. I keep myself equally informed about his syndrome and his needs. I am willing to have a face-to-face meeting to discuss particular foods and items we use with Ben, if you think that would be helpful.

This is *brief*. It is *informative* and reminds Angelina that Frank is equally informed about the child's particular condition. It is *friendly*, and Frank does not get defensive about Angelina's arguably insulting style. And it is *firm*, making it clear that Frank has the same information, and he reminds Angelina that he is as equally informed as she is.

## Conclusion

In this chapter, we have discussed many healthcare examples. This is the area of some of the most important communication regarding your child's well-being and future. Many coparents have a lot of trouble in this area because they are truly anxious about their child and want to take good care of him or her. So, using BIFF communications can be essential to cooperation and fast action when necessary.

In addition, how you cooperate about these important communications and decisions will make a big impact on your child. Seeing that you can jointly solve big problems will reassure your child and also teach him or her how to solve their own big problems as they grow up. BIFF communications are one of the easiest ways to manage your own stress while taking care of the predictable and unpredictable healthcare needs that your child is bound to have.

Generally, when parents have joint legal custody, it usually means that you communicate about healthcare decisions in advance of taking healthcare action, except in emergencies. Even though you may dread communicating with your coparent, it can save a lot of future conflict and stress to just send a simple BIFF communication on these matters. And if you have time, have someone review your BIFF before you send it so that it can be most effective.

# CHAPTER SEVEN

# BIFFs About Activities

One of the ways that parents help their children grow and develop is by involving them in activities. Activities cover a wide range of involvement, from infant swim classes to finishing scouting requirements, from organized sports to preparing entries in the county or state fair, from piano lessons to youth groups for religious education. Activities provide opportunities for children to develop many different skills, to practice the standards of our culture, and to build relationships with peers, and with adults.

Involving children in activities offers parents the opportunity to engage with their children at many different levels. Parents are able to share their love of the activity itself, as they coach a sport, or take their children fishing, or involve children in playing musical instruments alongside them. Activities give children the opportunity to develop skills, to practice, and to perform in a very short time span, where more formal education can take years for skills to develop to the point of real-world performance.

Activities also give parents who are coparenting opportunities to cooperate with one another in setting some policies to help guide their decision-making. Policies provide guidance so that some decisions can apply to several different situations over time.

# A Soccer Example

In this example, the mother, Nette, was a successful athlete through to the end of her education, playing soccer on scholarship in a midlevel university. She valued many aspects of her experience, but as she prepared to put her own daughters, Anya (age 5) and Mira (age 3) into activities, she wanted to set some boundaries. She sent the following message to the children's father, Reynaldo.

> Naldo,
>
> I hope you are having a wonderful weekend with the girls. They have been so excited to see your parents and show them what each of them can do with a soccer ball.
>
> I have been thinking about signing the kids up for soccer this spring, but before I do, I would like to suggest a couple of guiding principles that we might consider for all of the activities the kids are in. I have talked to coaches and former players alike, about their experience of sports while growing up. And as a former player myself, I think I have some important input to offer on this subject. There are many reasons for kids to be involved in sports, and frankly all sorts of things. And of course, we want to support our children in developing in the sports or music, or well, anything that they might show interest in. One of the important

things that kids learn from these kinds of activities is to stick to something, to play all the way through to the end, whether it be to the end of the play, the end of the game, or the end of the season.

Another concern that I have is about kids who have so much to do that they lose the joy of being in the activity. Now with living in two homes, I think they kids have a lot to deal with just going back and forth between our homes. And they have to keep up with all their stuff. Add to that the homework they will have to do, the equipment they will have to move back and forth between our homes, remembering what they are supposed to do on what day, and who is taking care of them each day. It is just a lot. So, I think that we should consider only allowing them to be in one activity at a time, or maybe one sport and an instrument when they show an interest in music, and maybe a one social group like scouts or church.

I am sorry for being so long-winded and getting this to you so late, but I would like to get these proposals ironed out and agreed to before we start the kids in activities.

I think that the money for soccer is due next week and the practices start the week after that.

Hope you are well,

Nette

Okay let's take a look at how Nette did.

# BIFF CHECKER

---

**Brief?** (2-5 sentences)  ☐ Yes
                                  ☑ No
                                  ☐ Maybe

Nette's message may be many things, but it is certainly not brief.

---

**Informative?** (Who, what, when, where, what for?)
                                  ☐ Yes
                                  ☐ No
                                  ☑ Maybe

There is certainly information in Nette's message. But she is not clear about what problem she is trying to solve, and she does not offer clear proposals for solving the problem(s).

---

**Friendly?**                 ☑ Yes
                                  ☐ No
                                  ☐ Maybe

She opens with a pleasant greeting and closes with a friendly salutation. In between, her tone is gentle, engaging and nonconfrontational.

---

**Firm?**                     ☐ Yes
                                  ☑ No
                                  ☐ Maybe

Reynaldo will be hard-pressed to figure out what Nette is proposing. At the end she includes some clearer statements about money for soccer and a start date for the activity. But even that could cause confusion as Nette asked to have agreement before the children start in an activity and, well, it is hard to know what Reynaldo is being asked to agree with.

**Advice?**

Probably not. Some of it reads like parenting advice but it does not seem to be directed specifically at Reynaldo.

**Admonishments?**

There does not seem to be any direct criticism.

**Apologies?**  ☑ Yes
☐ No
☐ Maybe

Seemingly just to fill space but it could be taken as a friendly gesture and not as an apology to appease him.

Reynaldo took some time to ponder what he thinks Nette is trying to propose and attempts a BIFF response.

Nette,

Thank you for sending the message about developing some plans for our kids to be in activities. As I understand the proposals:

**Your proposal 1.** When we sign the kids up for an activity, we will require that they finish that particular commitment. So, if it's a sport, they will be required to finish the season. If they sign up for an art class, they finish all of the sessions that have been paid for. If they are cast in a role for a play, they must stay with it until the performances of the play are over.

**Your proposal 2.** We will limit the number of activities that either of the children are in at any given time.

If I am right about what you are proposing, I agree to both of these proposals. I would like to make the following proposals in response.

**My proposal 1.** When we are preparing to sign the kids up for anything, we put in writing all of the things about that activity including how long it will go on, the cost, that we both sign it, and have the kids 'sign it' too.

**My proposal 2.** I propose that we start with one activity at a time for each of the girls and then talk about how they are doing with that one before we add another. (I agree that they will likely be able to do more than one thing at a time. I want to make sure that we are challenging them without involving them in too much.)

So, for now, the one activity that the kids are in is soccer, which starts in two weeks. I have paid my portion of the fee using the online payment option.

My parents got them little team jerseys from the USA women's soccer team. I am sure they will want to show them off when they get back to you tonight.

Be well,

Reynaldo

Now let's take a look at how Reynaldo did.

# BIFF CHECKER

**Brief?** (2-5 sentences)
☐ Yes
☐ No
☑ Maybe

Although his message does not fit within the 2-5 sentence guideline, it is succinct and to-the-point. He does not ramble or go into long explanations of what he is thinking.

**Informative?** (Who, what, when, where, what for?)
☑ Yes
☐ No
☐ Maybe

It provides a much-improved understanding of Nette's proposals and offers two clear proposals of his own.

**Friendly?**
☑ Yes
☐ No
☐ Maybe

His message is quite friendly. He shows appreciation for Nette's proposal focuses attention on Nette's upcoming contact with their children.

---

**Firm?**

☑ Yes
☐ No
☐ Maybe

It is for the most part firm. His message offers three straight-forward proposals and acknowledges that the additional proposal will require some ongoing communication and co-operation.

---

**Advice?**

☐ Yes
☑ No
☐ Maybe

It does not.

---

**Admonishments?**

☐ Yes
☐ No
☑ Maybe

This one is a bit tricky. Nette's message was long-winded and somewhat confusing. By offering back a synopsis of her proposals, Reynaldo might be perceived as being critical. He was careful not to offer criticism of her message as he offered his take on her proposals. He stayed focused on how best to move forward with making agreements that will benefit his children.

**Apologies?**
☐ Yes
☑ No
☐ Maybe

## Some Additional Thoughts

In the business of raising children together, neither parent is looking to be supervised by the other parent. Offering performance reviews of the other parent's work is unwelcome. We think you will find that the other parent will work better with you when you don't slip criticism into your messages.

Kids benefit from cooperation between parents when participating in activities. Anytime a child experiences both parents at a location at the same time there is the opportunity for anxiety, but there is also the opportunity for the child to experience parents cooperating with each other. Activities such as sports, musical and theater performances, and celebrations of achievements can create the environment for children to see parents trying to get along.

These public events with your children are exactly the situations for which we have learned to be polite. Wikipedia has a definition of polite that seems appropriate to these situations. "Politeness is the practical application of good manners or etiquette so as not to offend others." BIFF communication fits well with the practical application of good manners.

# Shared Sporting Events Example

In this next example, Rajiv is hoping to encourage better behavior between himself and his ex-wife Adeline when the two of them are at the same sports events with their children. Let's see how he does:

(Rajiv) We have an agreement that each parent brings the snacks and drinks to the games when it is their parenting time. Stop bringing them on my time. Stop. You need to see a therapist. Something is really, really wrong with you. Just stop. Have a good day.

Rajiv seems to want to send a BIFF message but there is obviously room for improvement. Let's take a look.

## BIFF CHECKER

**Brief?** (2-5 sentences) ☑ Yes
☐ No
☐ Maybe

It is definitely brief, but once we have taken out the problematic parts, it may be too brief.

---

**Informative?** (Who, what, when, where, what for?)

☑ Yes
☐ No
☐ Maybe

Rajiv is clear about his proposal.

---

**Friendly?**

☐ Yes
☑ No
☐ Maybe

Although he gives a nod to friendliness by suggesting that Adeline have a good day, his tone is directive, insulting and excessively assertive.

---

**Firm?**

☑ Yes
☐ No
☐ Maybe

It is firm but it is also harsh. The Firm part of BIFF is supposed to be a gentle end to the hostility, not part of it. Rajiv is clearly frustrated and his message will almost certainly cause Adeline to be defensive.

---

**Advice?**

☑ Yes
☐ No
☐ Maybe

He advises her to see a therapist. Whether or not she needs to see a therapist, it is none of us business and this is not the way to encourage her to do so.

**Admonishments?**  
☑ Yes  
☐ No  
☐ Maybe

His suggestion that she see a therapist and stating that something is wrong with her is very critical. He took the focus away from solving the snack problem and made the problem about Adeline. In fact, it's downright nasty and insulting.

**Apologies?**  
☐ Yes  
☑ No  
☐ Maybe

Now let's see how Adeline responds to Rajiv.

> (Adeline) You are impossible to work with!!! The kids hate, hate, hate, the snacks you bring. They are embarrassed that you just can't possibly pass up the opportunity to talk about your "healthy food." You are just angry because I bring snacks that the kids actually like. Everyone on the team likes it that I bring better snacks than you. Why don't you grow up and stop making everything always be about you and how special you are!

Well, that didn't go well. Let's try rebooting this conversation and see if a little coaching for Rajiv might help with their exchange. How would you suggest that Rajiv write his initial email on this subject? Give it a try but remember to check your response to see if it's Brief, Informative, Friendly and Firm. Also, see if it includes any admonishments, advice, or apologies. You can also practice at www.ConflictPlaybook.com.

How did you do? See what you think of this message:

> (Rajiv) Hey Adeline, hope you are doing well. I would like to get some help from you in managing the amount of snacks and drinks the kids are getting when it is my responsibility to bring them to the game. My memory is that at our last mediation we agreed that we would each only bring snacks and drinks for the team and for our kids when it is our own parenting time. Please respect that agreement. Thank you for the help with this. See you at the games on Saturday.

## BIFF CHECKER

**Brief?**

☑ Yes
☐ No
☐ Maybe

**Informative?**

☑ Yes
☐ No
☐ Maybe

**Friendly?**

☑ Yes
☐ No
☐ Maybe

**Firm?**

☑ Yes
☐ No
☐ Maybe

It is, but without being rude. He makes it end the conversation.

**Advice?**

☐ Yes
☑ No
☐ Maybe

**Admonishments?**

☐ Yes
☑ No
☐ Maybe

**Apologies?**

☐ Yes
☑ No
☐ Maybe

The focus of the message is on the problem to be solved, not on either of the parents involved. By keeping the message short and positive, Rajiv offers less opportunity for conflict, and if both parents can live by their agreements, the chances of conflict at the public events are reduced. Now the parents can simply be polite, enjoy their children's games and stay focused on cooperation.

# Conclusion

This chapter has shown several common issues that come up regarding the children's sporting events and coparent cooperation. We know this often doesn't go very well but these examples show how they can be handled better using BIFF communication.

We recognize that some parents can't both attend their children's sporting events because one or both are unable to restrain themselves from creating a conflict and embarrassing or highly distressing their children. In such situations, it is often better to simply avoid such conflicts by agreeing to respect each other's separate involvement with sports activities. However, this still may involve some communication, such as about when practices and games are on the other parent's time.

In some cases, one parent is involved in the sport, such as being a coach, while the other parent delivers and picks up the child. In other cases, they take turns being at practices and games. In yet other cases they can both attend but one remains in the distance and just watches without trying to interact with the child. All of this may involve important communication and planning. BIFF can help in all of these situations.

# CHAPTER EIGHT

# BIFFs About Finances

One of the more difficult topics that parents often have to communicate about is the allocation of resources. Two primary ways that we allocate resources are through the use of time and money, which parents often communicate about. Both are limited. Bottom line, coparents must decide how they will raise children together *within* limitations.

Talking about limitations can often trigger defensive feelings even within parents who by and large get along. When coparenting with someone who is no longer, or never was, a sweetheart, talking about the limitations on time and money is exactly the time to use BIFF messages.

## BIFF Communications About Time

Parents seem to be able to understand boundaries about meddling with the other parent's time much more effectively than they do with money. When providing guidelines and structures to help support families, we are much clearer, firmer, and more definitive in drawing the boundaries and guidelines for time.

There is a limit on how much time any of us have and

how much we can do in the time that we have available. The gift with time is that it is so plain. That does not mean that how we work with time is always clear. People speak of time management, which is just a way to muddy our thinking. It is not possible, even a little, to manage time. Time moves forward at a constant and unchanging pace and nothing we do has any influence on that. We simply cannot manage time. However, we can manage our calendars and we can become more efficient with what we are doing and when we are doing it.

So there is at least the possibility of some clarity in communication about time. We can agree, or impose, guidelines about how parents will interact about time. We set transfer times and consequences for being late. We develop elaborate systems for parents to use in trading time and we encourage parents to maintain boundaries so that limits on time are respected and maintained.

## A Lateness Example

There are many instances when coparents will need to communicate about time. Let's take a look at the example provided to us by Julian and Jenni.

### Jenni's first draft to Julian (not sent):

Hello Julian,

Well, I guess we are going to have to go back to court. I can't seem to get your attention any other way. You are late all the time, with everything. Not only can you not have the children ready to go when I come to pick them up, you can't get your vacation plans to me by the deadline. And sure, I know, I know, I could just move on with planning my vacations, but when I do, you throw a fit about not getting to have the vacation times that you want, on your years. Really, you need to see someone about this. It is a chronic problem that causes you problems everywhere. Didn't you get fired from that one job over being late all the time? Doesn't matter, I am sick of it and am contacting my attorney.

Have a nice day, and see you in court.

Let's take a look at how Jenni did.

## BIFF CHECKER

**Brief?**

☐ Yes
☐ No
☑ Maybe

It is not too terribly long, but it is longer than the recommended 2-5 sentences. Length is not really the big problem with Jenni's message.

---

**Informative?** (Who, what, when, where, what for?)

☐ Yes
☑ No
☐ Maybe

Mostly this message is a rant. Jenni appears to be so frustrated that she is having a hard time staying focused. The message could be shortened by staying focused on the one problem that she is trying to solve—getting information about Julian's summer vacation plans for himself and the children, Julie and Jack. And Jenni doesn't offer a proposal for a clear solution to that problem. Instead, she says that the decision-making will have to be turned over to someone else.

**Friendly?**

It appears that it has been a long time since Jenni has reviewed her BIFF book. She says hello and goodbye, but her tone is adversarial, and threatening someone with court is just never perceived as friendly.

**Firm?**

Because Jenni doesn't offer a proposal, it is hard to see what she is being firm about.

**Advice?**

☑ Yes
☐ No
☐ Maybe

Jenni's frustration has caused her to suggest seeking help from others, including therapists and judges. But, as we know, advising Julian to see someone is not likely to be well received, now will it provide the moment of illumination that guides him to seek help.

**Admonishments?** ☑ Yes
                    ☐ No
                    ☐ Maybe

This message could be characterized as one long admonishment.

**Apologies?** ☐ Yes
                ☑ No
                ☐ Maybe

We have one place of celebration for Jenni's message. She did not apologize for anything in the message.

Lucky for Julian, Jenni took her message to her coach (see Chapter 11) who helped her think through what she was trying to accomplish with her message to Julian. After a couple of times of writing, reviewing, and rewriting, the message that she sent was much improved.

> **Jenni's final draft to Julian (should she send it?):**
>
> Julian,
>
> I hope you are doing well. I am trying to make plans for time off with Julie and Jack this summer along with summer camps and other activities. I noticed in reviewing our parenting plan that this is your year to choose vacation times first. I will need to see yours before I provide my vacation dates to you in 13 days. I propose that you email your vacation dates to me no

later than this coming Friday, March 5, at midnight. Regardless, I will provide you with my vacation dates by March 15, at midnight, and expect that they will be honored.

Thank you for helping make plans for the kids for this summer.

Be well,

Jenni

Now it is your turn. Please take a few moments and carefully assess how Jenni did this time. Should she send it?

Is it brief? (2-5 sentences)

---

Is it informative?
(Who, what, when, where, what for?)

---

Is it friendly?

---

Is it firm?

---

Does it contain advice?

---

Does it contain admonishments?

---

Does it contain apologies?

---

Should she send it? Is it a good BIFF? We think so, although three edits might make it even better:

1. She doesn't really need this sentence, "I will need to see yours before I provide my vacation dates to you in 13 days", since she includes dates for him to send his to her, before she sends hers to him, which is already part of their parenting plan.

2. She doesn't really need the word "Regardless" when giving her date. This isn't necessary to her information and implies that he will be irresponsible, which he may react defensively to.

3. She doesn't really need the phrase "and expect that they will be honored." That should be a given and rubbing it in may also feel like an admonishment or insult to Julian, who may become less cooperative rather than more cooperative.

What do you think? Does it read better now?

**Jenni's final *final* draft to Julian (should she send it?):**

Julian,

I hope you are doing well. I am trying to make plans for time off with the Julie and Jack this summer, along with summer camps and other activities. I noticed, in reviewing our parenting plan, that this is your year to choose vacation times first. I propose that you email your vacation dates to me no later than this coming Friday, March 5, at midnight. I will provide you with my vacation dates by March 15, at midnight.

Thank you for helping make plans for the kids for this summer.

Be well,

Jenni

Which do you like better? Remember, it's up to the BIFF writer to make the final decision. If this was your BIFF, whichever one you preferred you could send.

The example above is just one of the many ways that coparents have to work together to manage time. And even in that example there are additional time concerns that may need proposals and agreements. Staying clear about the problem that is to be solved will certainly help bring resolution with less conflict.

## BIFF Communications about Money

Attempts to problem-solve about issues related to money can prove challenging for even the most experienced BIFF writer. Money is talked about all the time in one context or another. However, it is a subject that is rarely talked about when it comes down to an individual's or a family's day-to-day practices.

Thinking well about money is often clouded, as shown by these common scenarios and discussions:

- Parents regularly use this phrase: *living on a fixed income*. The implication is that there are those that do not live on a fixed income. In fact, almost everyone has limited resources.

- It is not uncommon that people enter into divorce with the idea that they will be able to maintain two households at the pre-divorce standard of living, using the same amount of money that they had available when operating one household. Paying for two homes, two sets of utilities, rents or mortgages, twice the numbers of vacation, and so forth, of course costs more.

- Money will make up for the emotional pain of the divorce . . . many people think. Well, no. Money just makes for the ability to pay for more stuff, but it does little to help with healing after divorce.

The lesson here is that clarity is crucial when coparents are trying to work together on money-related matters. BIFF communications are a really good way to reduce conflict so you can concentrate on parenting.

## A Paying for Activities Example

Let's look at the communication between Andrei and his coparent, Elizabeth. Andrei is preparing to respond to the message he recently received from Elizabeth about paying for fall activities for their children, Blaze and Portia.

> Andrei, I know you don't give a damn about being on time with paying me for stuff. But I am going to need for you to get me paid up for the kid's activities and healthcare. It is the beginning for soccer for both Blaze and Portia, and I signed them up for the Kick'em Hard Premier League. You owe me **$1500** for the sign-up fees. There are also coaching fees due by the end of the week. Your part of that will be another **$500**. And Blaze had a growth spurt so he is going to need new shin guards and cleats. Just include that money at the same time. And scouts started last week, and the money was due, so I had to pay that too. Add in another **$100** to cover your part of scouts. And you are also behind in paying me for the kid's recent physicals and other medical expenses. I am tired of being a bank for you. You know that I have bills to pay for your kids, and you are busy spending money on your girlfriend and her

kids. Get your act together and start caring about your own kids.

Whew! It's pretty clear that this isn't a BIFF communication but let's focus on how Andrei could respond to this.

Elizabeth, thank you for taking care of getting the kids signed up for activities this season. I am going to try to be clear about what I am paying, for what, and what I need to be able to pay additionally.

You and I agreed that we would sign the kids up for regular Play Hard – Have Fun Soccer League. I have included what would half of the cost of signing the kids up to play there, like I said I would: $450.

PH-HF SL does not pay the coaches, so I have included nothing for coaching fees.

I have noticed that both Blaze and Portia need new gear, and I plan to take them to the sporting goods store and outfit them this weekend when they are with me. I have coupons for the name brand gear they have been asking about, and should be able to get some good deals, so I won't need you to reimburse me for those expenses.

For the other activity expenses, of course I am willing to pay for anything that we have agreed to in advance, in writing, on the online communication service. I will just need to get receipts showing what has been paid.

I see that you have posted documentation of the medical expenses on the service, so I have included money to cover my portion: $393.13.

The total amount sent to your account is: $843.13.

Again, thank you for taking care of getting the kids signed up, and for taking them to their physicals and other medical appointments.

Hope you have a great time with the kids this weekend.

Andrei

How did Andrei do? Let's take a look.

## BIFF CHECKER

**Brief?**    ☐ Yes
            ☑ No
            ☐ Maybe

However, the message that Elizabeth sent covered so much that it is difficult to respond in just 5 sentences. He does a good job of staying focused just on the problems that need to be solved, who owes what, and under what circumstances.

**Informative?** (Who, what, when, where, what for?)

☑ Yes
☐ No
☐ Maybe

Andrei provides clarity about what he is paying, for what reasons, and what more he is willing to pay, and under what circumstances.

**Friendly?**        ☑ Yes
                     ☐ No
                     ☐ Maybe

Andrei maintains a fairly friendly tone throughout the message, even though he is saying "no" to some aspects of the expenses Elizabeth requested. He does not get pulled into the personal attacks.

**Firm?**            ☑ Yes
                     ☐ No
                     ☐ Maybe

Andrei responds firmly by reminding Elizabeth of their agreements and proceeds with paying in accordance with the agreements. In doing so, he maintains good boundaries and at the same time provides what he can for his children. In other words, it isn't firm *harsh*, but rather firm *clarity* and firm *ending* of the conversation.

**Advice?**          ☐ Yes
                     ☑ No
                     ☐ Maybe

It certainly could have. Andrei really wanted to suggest to Elizabeth that she just do what they agreed to, so she would not be in the situation of paying for so much of the expense for soccer on her own. However, he was not asked to offer an opinion about what could make their financial interactions better, so he left well enough alone.

**Admonishments?** ☐ Yes
☑ No
☐ Maybe

Again, no, not that. Andrei didn't want to criticize Elizabeth, in fact he had to take out several sentences that he wrote into the first draft. But he realized that he is not Elizabeth's supervisor and his suggestions would not help.

**Apologies?** ☐ Yes
☑ No
☐ Maybe

Clear, brief, friendly communication goes a long way in making decisions about money. As we mentioned previously, too much talking just provides more opportunities for conflict. Staying focused on the problem that is to be solved allows for solutions to be more apparent.

# Conclusion

Money can be a big source of conflict and bad communication filled with Blamespeak. As these examples show, it is possible to stay focused on what to do now, rather than going into the past or implying irresponsibility for the coparent. Many parents develop systems for joint activities and joint medical expenses. Since these come up over and over again, a system can help reduce the communication and risks of miscommunication. Such systems often include jointly agreeing in writing to activities and whether there is agreement to share the cost. Also, reimbursing medical costs within thirty days is another frequent agreement, so things don't get lost or behind.

You can use BIFF communications to discuss your system, then you can keep future BIFFs very brief as you implement your system, whatever it is.

# CHAPTER NINE

# BIFFs About Changes to Plans and Schedules

Changed plans and calendar changes are challenging even for parents who get along very well. When parents don't communicate well to start with, or when one parent is high conflict, calendar changes can cause great distress.

Sometimes calendar changes are crucial and must be requested. Sometimes a change of plans is optional and done only for the benefit of one person. Remember the characteristics of high conflict people from Chapter 1 (and remember to *never say* you think your coparent is one or it will make things worse for days, months or years):

**All-or-nothing thinking**
(one person is all good, another is all bad)
**Unmanaged emotions** (exaggerated anger, fear, sadness—out of proportion to events)
**Extreme behavior** (yelling, hitting, lying, spreading rumors, impulsive actions, etc.)
**Preoccupation with blaming others** (people close to them or people in authority).

If your parenting plan is in writing and is detailed, as it should be, trying to make changes to it runs into conflicts with a high conflict person's likely rigid, all-or-nothing thinking. If the parenting plan is good in their eyes, any change to it must be bad in their eyes. If you originally insisted on a detailed parenting plan in order to manage the other party who you perceive to be a high conflict person, that detailed plan may be used against you. And if you're trying to change the plan, even in a small way, you may be blamed, even if the reason for your change isn't your fault.

Many parents simply want *flexibility* from the other parent. While flexibility in life is generally a good thing, it's generally not a good thing when it comes to parenting with a high conflict coparent.

## Temporary, One-Time Changes

Things happen. You may have completely screwed up and told the other parent the wrong dates for your summer vacation with the kids.

Wendy made certain to send Robert her vacation dates by the time their parenting plan said they were due. She knew if she missed that deadline, Robert would try to use it as an excuse to disallow a summer vacation. Then she received her confirmations from the airline and the hotel, and she had booked an entirely different week. She can't modify the hotel and flight arrangements without losing a lot of money. And Robert hasn't chosen his vacation week yet, but Wendy knows if he hears of her dilemma, he'll deliberately choose the week she needs. How does Wendy tell Robert she made a mistake and needs to change the vacation, without apologizing and putting herself at risk?

# A Summer Vacation Example

Wendy starts with a BIFF email:

**Wendy to Robert:** *I know I sent you our vacation dates, and upon checking things, those dates were wrong.* (She hasn't apologized, but she's acknowledged a mistake.) *I need to change those dates from July 6-13 to July 13-20 instead. As I know you haven't chosen your summer dates yet, this shouldn't be a problem. I appreciate your understanding and making this change. I look forward to receiving your summer dates.* (She is firm and friendly.)

Robert, the higher-conflict personality, responds as Wendy expects:

**Robert to Wendy:** *You're an idiot if you think I'm going to let you monkey around with dates like this. I was just about to notify you of my dates, and they are July 13-20. I'm taking these dates and you can't do anything about it, because I have it in writing that you wanted a different time. You always think you can do whatever you want, but you're not getting away with it this time. You've always been disorganized and sloppy and this just shows your true colors. Have a fun time July 6-13.*

Wendy is ready for this with another BIFF response.

**Wendy to Robert:** *I was able to make the change of dates before your dates were chosen, so there is no harm to you from the change. If by some chance you have something showing that you had paid non-refundable money before you received my notice, please send me that and we can talk about how to reimburse you. Our email exchanges are clear that I made this change of dates timely, and I will do whatever is necessary to enforce the July 13-*

*20 dates. Our children will be able to have enjoyable vacations with both of us this summer!*

Will the BIFF response solve everything? Maybe, or maybe not. But Wendy is brief, informative, firm (she will enforce the times she needs) and even friendly in emphasizing that these vacations are primarily for the children. She focuses on the children and not her own needs, but recognizes that if Robert has spent money, they can talk about reimbursement. (She's anticipating he hasn't spent any.) Hopefully she doesn't need the help of the court to enforce her revised vacation dates, but if she does, her BIFF responses should help a judge see that she tried to resolve this problem.

## A Trading Weekends Example

Sometimes the need for a change isn't the parent's fault at all. Family or outside forces may plan big events during time assigned to the other parent.

Holly's sister announced her engagement in the spring, setting a June 5 wedding date. Holly immediately checked her calendar and found out the kids' father, Ryan, was scheduled to have the kids that weekend. It's only March at this point so Holly hopes the weekends can be switched as everyone wants the kids to attend their aunt's wedding.

> (Holly) I just found out Colleen's wedding is set for June 5, so I am asking that we trade weekends to make sure I have the children from June 2-6 for celebrations going on with the wedding. This is very important to my family and you know how close Colleen is with the kids, and Colleen would be devastated if the kids couldn't attend. As that is your scheduled weekend with the kids, we can trade a weekend. It's only March, so you shouldn't have any objection. The kids are very excited about Aunt Colleen's wedding. Don't you think this is a great opportunity for them?

How did Holly do?

## BIFF CHECKER

| **Brief?** | ☐ Yes |
| --- | --- |
| | ☑ No |
| | ☐ Maybe |

It's not as brief as it could be and the extra sentences about how important this is to Holly's family and that Colleen would be "devastated" probably isn't necessary.

**Informative?** (Who, what, when, where, what for?)

☐ Yes
☐ No
☑ Maybe

There is no mention of where the wedding is, so Ryan will possibly wonder if the children will be traveling that weekend. It would be helpful to include "The wedding is here in town so we won't be traveling."

**Friendly?**

☐ Yes
☑ No
☐ Maybe

It focuses on Holly and her family and somewhat minimizes Ryan's interests.

**Firm?**

☐ Yes
☑ No
☐ Maybe

Leaving the last sentence open is not wise. Ryan may in fact *not* think this is a great opportunity for the children, and Ryan may not be very fond of Colleen.

Holly's email could be improved and made more BIFF by excluding the non-information about her family's feelings, leaving out the last sentence, and giving Ryan more details so he knows whether or not the children will be traveling. Do you think Ryan's response is BIFF?

> (Ryan) Not a chance I'm trading weekends with you. Colleen was a huge problem in our marriage and she's a terrible role model for the kids. No, it's not a great opportunity! The kids won't be at her wedding, and she can be "devastated" all she wants. I'll do whatever it takes to make sure the kids are anywhere else that weekend.

Was this a BIFF communication? Nope. While its Brief, it's not Informative and instead is judgmental and reactive. It's not Friendly and not Firm because it's a challenge rather than calmly ending the discussion so that Holly is certain to respond. Ryan, as a likely high conflict personality, shows his *all-or-nothing* thinking and took advantage of all the openings given to him by Holly's original email. He was able to take aim directly at Holly's family, Colleen, and respond to Holly's unnecessary question about it being a great opportunity. Holly's email left herself open to these attacks.

Holly could try and correct the situation with a follow-up email that is BIFF.

> (Holly) I forgot to let you know that the wedding is here in town so the children won't be traveling. Family events are important for our children, and I'm sure there will be events with your family you'll want to make sure they attend. Your response confirms that you don't already have plans for that weekend, so please let me know what weekend you'd like to trade.

Again, if Holly needs to take further action—such as seeking a court order—to make sure she has the children for this weekend, this email will help her show that she tried to be brief, informative, friendly, and firm in her request to Ryan.

## More Permanent, Long-Term Changes

Sometimes you need to suggest a long-term change in the schedule, such as switching who has the children for Christmas (even years to odd years), or changing an alternating weeks schedule so a parent has the opposite week. These discussions require a good BIFF communication from the start, as a permanent change to the schedule may proceed to mediation or court. The situation should be carefully managed from the very first communication.

# A Christmas Holiday Example

Wendy, who already made the mistake about her vacation dates earlier this year, now is engaged to a man who also has children from his prior marriage. They've realized that he has his children for Christmas Day in odd-numbered years, but Wendy has her children in even-numbered years! With these schedules, they will never have a Christmas with all their children together. Wendy needs to approach Robert about switching so that she has the children in odd-numbered years (which is this year).

Robert—I'm asking that you consider switching our Christmas schedule with the children so that I have them in odd-numbered years and you have them in even-numbered years. I realize I had them last year (an even-numbered year) and that this year would be your year with them. Please consider switching this, as we will have the exact same times with the children, just in different years. I'm hoping we can work this out between ourselves.

## BIFF CHECKER

---

**Brief?**  ☑ Yes
☐ No
☐ Maybe

She was very brief

**Informative?** (Who, what, when, where, what for?)

☑ Yes
☐ No
☐ Maybe

She was very informative about exactly what she was requesting.

**Friendly?**

☑ Yes
☐ No
☐ Maybe

She was friendly and said please.

**Firm?**

☑ Yes
☐ No
☐ Maybe

She was firm as she said she'd like to work it out between themselves but left open the possibility that they might have to get others involved. Strategically, she did not do two things: (1) she did not say this is because of her fiancé's children's schedule; and (2) she did not make an offer to give Robert two Christmases in a row in order to try and seal the deal. She left that possibility open in order to see how he responds.

**Robert doesn't disappoint. He responds:**

(Robert) Wendy, you've got to be kidding me?!? What a transparent attempt for you to have the kids two Christmases in a row. You know you had them last year and now you want them this year too --- funny how you couldn't ask me last year right before it was YOUR time with them. No, you can't have the kids for two Christmases in a row. I was without them last year, and this year we have plans to go to Illinois for Christmas.

**Was this a BIFF?** No. It was brief, but not straight information, not friendly and not firm. Let's see how Wendy handles this.

(Wendy) I completely understand that you want to have the kids this Christmas. If you are willing to do this trade-off, I will agree that you still have them this year (an odd-numbered year), and you will have them again next year (even-numbered), so it's you that has them two years in a row. After that, we would start the odd-year to me, even year to you. Let's confirm that arrangement.

Wendy's response is brief and informative, friendly and accommodating to Robert's interests, and firm: "Let's confirm." She did not argue with him or rise to his level of anger that she's trying to take his children away from him. Ideally, this compromise proposal will resolve the issue. If not, she can decide whether it's worth taking this issue back to court. At least her emails have been brief, informative, friendly and firm.

## Starting Difficult Negotiations with the Right Tone

Trying to change more of the schedule will be trickier. If the parents have an alternating weeks schedule (or something that's called a 5/2/2/5, where one parent always has the children on Mondays and Tuesdays, and the other parent always has Wednesdays and Thursdays), trying to switch to the opposite week or opposite days is not easy. Parents tend to make plans based on the existing schedule. But a parent may find that his or her circumstances change, so that a parent is now working too much on the days he or she has the children. Or, a new spouse may have children on exactly the opposite schedule and some effort is needed to coordinate the schedules. A BIFF request can start the negotiations with the right tone.

## A Switching Nights Example

In this case, David hasn't studied BIFF. His request is somewhat abrupt.

> Karen, we need to change our schedule as I need to be the Wednesday-Thursday parent. I now have a much greater workload on Mondays and Tuesdays including things that keep me late through the dinner hour. Also, I've noticed that the kids have way more homework on Mondays and Tuesdays and that's just not fair to have that all done at my house. There's no reason you can't do Mondays and Tuesdays with your work schedule although you'll probably try to think of some reason just to make my life harder.

## BIFF CHECKER

| | |
|---|---|
| **Brief?** | ☐ Yes |
| | ☐ No |
| | ☑ Maybe |

He was somewhat brief.

---

**Informative?** (Who, what, when, where, what for?)

☐ Yes
☑ No
☐ Maybe

He was not very informative. He could have explained what about his work has changed so much. Without explanation, Karen may ascertain that it's really about the homework.

---

**Friendly?**

☐ Yes
☑ No
☐ Maybe

He's not friendly and in fact insults Karen while asking for a favor.

---

**Firm?**

☐ Yes
☑ No
☐ Maybe

Although it is firm, it's the wrong kind of firm. He's rigid and harsh. Firm is supposed to mean that you calmly end the conversation or ask for an answer to two choices.

Karen still has some bitterness from prior to and during the divorce when she was constantly expected to change her schedule to accommodate David's work hours and *dinners*. Her first thought is to respond like this:

David:

My days of bending every which way to accommodate your work schedule (including sleeping with your employees) are over. We are divorced and you are on your own. It's tough when someone else expects you to change your schedule, isn't it? Well I'm done. You need to figure out how to manage your life, get kids' homework done, and manage your own work schedule—women do it all the time.

But Karen has read this book and she knows that a BIFF response will serve her children better. Admonishing David and giving advice won't have any effect on him. She takes a few deep breaths and responds in a BIFF way:

David:

I have made many plans with the children that are based on me having them on Wednesdays and Thursdays. One of those things is having Helen in dance immediately after school every Wednesday from 3:15-4:30. I can consider modifying some of the things we do, as long as you agree that Helen remains in dance and that you will always get her from dance at 4:30 on Wednesdays. Also, we have already made plans for the following dates: Thursday August 13, Thursday September 10, and Thursday October 15, from after school until 6:30pm. So long as you agree regarding Helen's dance and that I will have the children on those three dates, we can switch our weekdays starting on

Monday August 27. The weekend of August 24-26 is yours, and you would take the children to school on August 27, I would pick them up after school that day, and the schedules would switch then. If these terms are acceptable, please confirm by return email.

Karen has considered her response and determined that changing the schedule would be okay, so long as she gets certain considerations.

## BIFF CHECKER

**Brief?**
☐ Yes
☐ No
☑ Maybe

Her email is not particularly brief, but it's as brief as it can be in order to be informative with the specific dates involved.

**Informative?**
☑ Yes
☐ No
☐ Maybe

**Friendly?**
☑ Yes
☐ No
☐ Maybe

It is friendly enough (more businesslike than friendly).

**Firm?**

☑ Yes
☐ No
☐ Maybe

David should be clear upon reading this that unless he agrees to the terms, Karen is not likely to agree to the switch he needs.

Importantly, she didn't make fun of David's reluctance to do a lot of homework and didn't admonish him or try to argue that the homework allocation "isn't fair." Arguing about that issue wouldn't be informative and likely wouldn't convince David anyway. And, she didn't try to give him advice about doing homework or managing his work hours better.

Finally, parents sometimes have to deal with a high conflict coparent who agrees to one thing in the parenting plan and then wants to change it, and a BIFF response is necessary to control those communications.

## A First Right of Caretaking Example

Todd agreed to, and in fact insisted on, a first right of caretaking provision (also known as "Right of First Refusal") in the final parenting plan. He felt this would be a good way for him to keep tabs on Jen and know when she wasn't personally watching the kids or know when she went out on a date. He insisted that the provision state that any time a parent was not watching the children for a period of five hours or more, the other parent had to be asked first if he or she wanted to watch the children. Jen didn't want this but finally agreed just to get the case settled.

That provision hasn't worked out the way Todd thought. Jen seems to be home with the kids most of the time, and although she has a new boyfriend, they tend to spend their evenings at home with the kids when she has them, and she freely dates when Todd has the children. Todd, on the other hand, has started being more social and playing more golf, and he wants to do those things even when he has the children. But every time he goes out he has to call and offer Jen the chance to care for them first. Jen almost always says "yes" —it seems that she and her boyfriend really like being with the kids! Todd would now prefer to be able to keep the kids at his home with a nanny during his parenting time.

Todd, in his usual way, approaches Jen like this:

Jen—

The first right of refusal isn't reasonable now, so we need to cancel it. We should each be able to leave the kids with whatever sitter we want. The kids are sick and tired of having to come to your house all the time. I've talked to a bunch of other divorced people, and no one has that requirement in their court orders. It's kind of ridiculous that you baby the kids like this. Plus, you never ask me to take care of them on your time, and I know you go out, so it just means you're violating the agreement anyway.

Jen's response to this needs to be BIFF, as she would like to quash constant attempts to change things.

Todd: thank you for your email. I believe the first right of caretaking provision is working as it should and I'm very glad you had it added. All parts of our agreement are important. The kids love seeing their other parent and knowing who will be taking care of them. I am not interested in removing that provision.

If Todd continues to email her about this provision, Jen can keep sending the same email in response, as it covers the issue. She may want to re-think the small dig at Todd ("I'm very glad you had it added") because it does leave an opening for him to respond and claim it wasn't him.

# Conclusion

Major changes to a specific parenting time schedule are difficult to address and can't always be resolved with email exchanges. But most requests for schedule changes start in the ways mentioned here. The more BIFF communications that take place, the more likely a successful resolution will occur between coparents.

With these big decisions, such as switching the ongoing mid-week schedule, it may sometimes be necessary to go back to court or back to a Parenting Coordinator (who helps with scheduling decisions and communication between major court hearings). In either case, you want to be able to show a reasonable BIFF communication from your end.

# CHAPTER TEN

# BIFFs for Social Media

Social media is generally thought of as using the Internet, including apps, to allow the creation and sharing of content, or participation in social networking. Sites that immediately come to mind as social media include Facebook, Instagram, Snapchat, Twitter, LinkedIn, TikTok, WhatsApp, YouTube and a host of others. Social media can also include all the *dating* sites, *rating* sites like Yelp and TripAdvisor, plus hundreds or thousands of online platforms that are popular outside the United States. Your children could name multiple social media sites that you've never heard of.

While it might be easiest to tell coparents not to use social media at all, that advice isn't practical. Some people do avoid social media, but if parents are already using it by the time of the separation, the use is likely to continue. It's also beneficial for a parent to be aware of social media in order to monitor the children's use.

Social media is not always bad for coparenting. Photo sharing is easier between parents (and extended family) through the use of Facebook, Instagram, and other free platforms. Pictures of your daughter at bat in baseball getting ready to swing can be sent to the other parent almost before she hits the ball and a full video of her rounding the bases can follow. Other apps are useful for communication between a parent and a child while playing games. And most of this use is entirely free.

Social media platforms created specifically for coparenting are of great assistance to parents. Those platforms seem to be less likely to be misused by high conflict people because they need and do better with lots of structure. When a platform is set up exclusively to talk about child issues, including review of the family activity calendar, the impetus to argue, insult, and disparage may be pacified. Or, being on a specialized email system makes it more obvious that a court could be reviewing the communication. Even high conflict people tend to be on their best behavior when using coparenting software.

Researchers have noted that communication through technology, rather than in-person or telephone communication, allows coparents a level of disengagement that can reduce conflict. The non-concurrent aspect of communication through email and social media platforms provides disengagement and *breathing room* which help reduce conflict.

Having noted all the positives about social media, this chapter addresses what to do about negative social media use between parents. Both parents are at risk of misusing social media occasionally. The biggest coparenting social media problems generally involve:

- Your post while really, really mad or emotional, or something that puts you in a bad parenting light
- Your coparent posts about new relationships in a taunting manner

- Your coparent posts negative comments and lies about you
- Your coparent posts embarrassing pictures of you
- Your coparent's new *special someone* posts about your children

## Posting While Really, Really Mad or Emotional, or Something That Puts You in a Bad Parenting Light

Posting while emotional is arguably the most dangerous (and sometimes the most entertaining) part of social media. Most apps are easily accessed, and typing or dictating statements that you'll regret later can be done in the true heat of the moment.

It is true that posts can be taken down later, after you've re-thought things. But before you can do that someone may have grabbed a screen shot of your post. Once something is on the Internet, it truly might be forever. If you post a picture of the hole your new boyfriend punched in the wall of your house, you can be sure it will show up in your custody hearing in a few weeks. A post about how hung over you were the night before will bolster claims that you drink excessively. Posts about where you are at a certain time may show you weren't home with the children.

**A note about deleting or cancelling things you have posted.** If you are involved in litigation including a divorce or custody matter, it can be a serious violation to *sanitize* your social media accounts and delete things you think might be harmful to you. Once court proceedings are started, any attempt to delete your earlier postings could tell the court you are hiding something and trying to destroy evidence.

Lawyers call this *spoliation of evidence*—and you do not want to be accused of that. You should consult with your attorney before you delete anything, deactivate an account, or entirely close a social media account when you're involved in litigation. There are federal rules about *electronically stored information* that you don't want to violate.

### If Your Ex Posts About the New Love of Her Life

If your ex thinks that posting about her new relationship is a good way to taunt you, the best answer is "Don't look." If you have friends telling you what your ex is posting or forwarding you pictures and posts, you should tell those friends you have no interest and ask them to stop. Responding to the pictures you don't like or posting comments on them will result in your negative comments being used against you in the future.

# Social Media Example

### What if your ex posts horrible things about you?

Susan knows her ex-husband, Wade, posts horrible things about her on Facebook. While she doesn't look at his accounts any more, they have several friends in common who tell her about his posts and send her screen shots. Wade frequently posts about Susan's parenting deficiencies, telling anyone who will listen that she leaves the children home alone, lets men sleep overnight when the kids are with her, and is drunk all the time. None of these things are true, but Susan wants to know how to handle Wade's lies.

If possible, Susan should collect whatever posts mention

her by name in order to show a judge how the other parent talks about her. She should not respond in kind, no matter how tempting. When a judge is hearing a parenting matter, posts like Wade's will put him in a very bad light. The judge's primary focus will be how each parent's behavior affects the children. In some jurisdictions, in considering the children's best interests, one factor is which parent is more likely to foster a good relationship between the children and the other parent. If Susan elects to fight fire with fire and responds by posting outrageous things about Wade on her social media, the behaviors of the parents cancel each other out and the judge will simply know he has two high conflict parents who can't put the children's interests first. Susan needs to take the high road.

If Susan feels it's necessary to talk about Wade's posts on her own page, she should keep it BIFF. Her friends will appreciate it.

**Susan Smith**
2 hours ago

Friends: Some of you know that my former spouse posts about me on his Facebook page. The things he says about me are not true and are meant to embarrass me. Anyone reading this knows me, so you know those things are not true. I am sorry you are exposed to his negativity. Please know that we both love our children, that I am doing my best to create a good environment for them and that I wish Wade the best.

Her post is brief, informative, friendly (and even upbeat), and firm. It does not invite further comment, although on social media, she is likely to get comments.

There is no reason for Susan to individually refute Wade's allegations, particularly if they are vague (that she's "always drunk").

If Wade has made a specific allegation on his Facebook posts that Susan feels should be responded to, Susan can address it briefly: "Wade posted that the Department of Child Safety was investigating me. This is not true and never has been true." which should put that issue to rest. Susan needs to realize, however, that by mentioning a specific allegation on her own page she may be spreading the rumor further and giving it more publicity. In general, however, when it is posted somewhere it can be helpful to quickly respond so that it does not become a serious rumor. In such a case it is ideal to respond on the same platform as the allegation, as explained in Chapter 2.

Some comments may come from Susan's own potential Negative Advocates (people who want to help, but actually make things worse) who try to get her to post something negative about Wade online. That kind of fight would be fun for some onlookers. Susan needs to make it clear to those Negative Advocates that she is not going to post anything negative and she'll continue to wish Wade well, as that's best for her children.

## If Your Ex Posts Explicit or Embarrassing Pictures of You

If the pictures posted are sexually explicit or nudes, you may have a cause of action and can file both a police report and a civil action for damages. You should seek legal advice. Many jurisdictions consider this stalking or cyberbullying and have specific criminal statutes covering this conduct. If the pictures posted are simply unflattering, these laws don't apply. In that case, the best advice is—don't look. You can contact the social media platform involved and ask if any references to your name that are associated with the picture can be removed. The "Report Abuse" section of a site can give you more information.

### If Your Ex's New Special Someone Posts with or About Your Children

You may become aware that a new boyfriend, girlfriend, fiancé or spouse is posting on social media, posing with your children. This is concerning to some parents, particularly because they don't know the extent to which the new relationship is making the children's pictures public. There is likely little that can be done if a third party is posting pictures of the children with the approval of one parent, but a BIFF communication can be attempted.

## Pictures of Your Children Example

Kendra and Toni have two children, ages 3 and 5, for whom they share parenting time. Toni has started living with Amy who loves the children. Amy posts pictures of herself with the two children constantly on her Facebook and Instagram pages, including pictures at the zoo, at their preschool, and while playing at parks and in their yard. Some of the pictures identify where the children go to preschool and some show the children in bathing suits. Kendra is concerned that (a)

Amy is way too enamored of her children, when Amy and Toni aren't even engaged at this point; and (b) that Amy's social media outlets may be disseminated far and wide and may be putting public pictures of her children in bathing suits out for anyone to see. Kendra has also read stories of online predators tracking down children where they live or go to school. Kendra wants the extensive use of her children's pictures to stop.

> Toni,
>
> I don't know who this Amy person thinks she is . . . but MY children aren't HERS. She acts on Facebook like they're hers, posting things like "The babies love their ice cream". They're not her babies! I gave birth to them and she will never be their mother. I've seen pictures of my 3-year old in a tiny bathing suit on her Instagram, and if I can see it, any pedophile can. Are you happy that some 60-year old pervert is looking at your daughter? And the name of their preschool is in some of her posts, so anyone can go to preschool and take my children. Your stupid slut of a girlfriend is putting our kids in danger and I'm going to make it stop if you won't. You've never cared a bit about their safety and wouldn't even use the car seats right until I brought it up in court.

Is Kendra's email a BIFF? Of course not! And it misses the mark and probably isn't going to make Toni want to help her. Let's check it.

# BIFF CHECKER

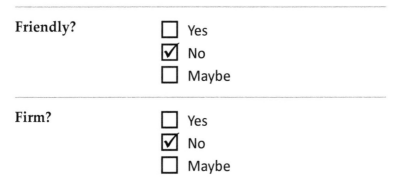

**Brief?**
☐ Yes
☑ No
☐ Maybe

**Informative?**
☐ Yes
☑ No
☐ Maybe

While it has some information, it has more emotion than anything else.

**Friendly?**
☐ Yes
☑ No
☐ Maybe

**Firm?**
☐ Yes
☑ No
☐ Maybe

She goes off on a tangent about car seats. It doesn't suggest a firm result or try to inform Toni about actual harm that might come to the children.

If Kendra can re-write her email to Toni in BIFF form, she has a better chance of getting a good result. How would you re-write her email?

Remember to check your response to see if it's Brief, Informative, Friendly and Firm. Also, don't forget to check if it includes any admonishments, advice, or apologies.

_____

_____

_____

_____

_____

_____

_____

_____

_____

_____

Now you can check your own BIFF.

# BIFF CHECKER

**Brief?** (2-3 sentences)  ☐ Yes
☐ No
☐ Maybe

**Informative?** (Who, what, when, where, what for?)
☐ Yes
☐ No
☐ Maybe

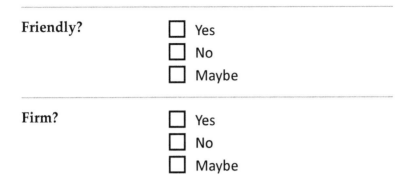

**Friendly?**  ☐ Yes
☐ No
☐ Maybe

**Firm?**  ☐ Yes
☐ No
☐ Maybe

How did you do? Feel free to try re-writing it again before you read this example:

> Toni,
>
> I'm happy for our children that they have someone like Amy who obviously likes being with them. I have some concerns about having the children's pictures on social media too much. I am careful with my own accounts to make sure that no one other than immediate friends can see my pictures of the children. I have read scary things about what people online do to see pictures of children and even find out where the children live or go to school. I know you care about our children, so I'm pointing out that if I can see their pictures on Amy's Instagram, probably anyone can (as we are not followers of each other). Would you ask Amy if she can make her social media accounts more private if she's going to post pictures of our children? I'm sure she would not want to do anything dangerous for them.

# BIFF CHECKER

| **Brief?** | ☐ Yes |
| | ☐ No |
| | ☑ Maybe |

While it has some information, it has more emotion than anything else.

| **Informative?** | ☑ Yes |
| | ☐ No |
| | ☐ Maybe |

It informs that Kendra is careful with her own social media and states what her specific concerns are. She addresses that she does not like the situation, but she does not personally attack Amy.

| **Friendly?** | ☑ Yes |
| | ☐ No |
| | ☐ Maybe |

The email is friendly and leaves out any jealousy or possessive comments that would spoil Kendra's message.

| **Firm?** | ☑ Yes |
| | ☐ No |
| | ☐ Maybe |

Kendra asks for solutions, which is more likely to get a positive response from Toni than the original attack.

# Conclusion

Social media adds complications to coparent communication because it potentially involves many other people, known and unknown. Communicating using the BIFF method may really help in discouraging inappropriate online activity, rather than escalating a coparent—especially a high conflict coparent—into publicly saying very nasty things or posting nasty photos.

More often, people just aren't thinking about the widespread implications of their posts. From creating evidence that can be used against you in court to exposing your children to unsavory strangers, it's always wise to have some agreements with your coparent about what the rules should be. That usually means initiating a discussion with a BIFF communication. Now you have some examples for addressing these risky issues. Emphasizing that you believe the other parent does not want to hurt the child or expose them to risks is a good message to include, as Kendra did in her second draft to Toni.

# SECTION

3

# CHAPTER ELEVEN

# Coaching for BIFF™

Becoming an effective communicator using BIFF is a process. First, you get familiar with the ideas involved in writing BIFF messages. Next, you understand their value in reducing conflict between coparents as well as increasing effective problem-solving. Then you commit to using the method. We have found that one of the most helpful ways to learn quickly and stay accountable is to have a coach and to be a coach. This chapter is included as a way of equipping anyone to coach others to write BIFF responses.

Showing your BIFF messages to a trusted spouse, friend or counselor before you send them is almost always a good idea. It slows you down just a bit, letting you think through your communication more thoroughly. It reminds you to be accountable for what you are saying and brings you back to thinking about BIFF as a part of each message. Having another person's feedback can, in the end, save you a lot of time, emotional upset, and maybe even a lot of money. Your coach can help remind you that the underlying principal in BIFF communication is to send messages that take into consideration an effort to avoid creating defensiveness in the receiving party, and to avoid your own defensiveness. You may want to find or create a good BIFF coach to help you if you struggle with responses.

Think through the people that you count on for good counsel. It could be your current sweetheart, one of your parents, a really good friend or your ongoing counselor. Start by explaining what you are trying to accomplish by changing your way of communicating. Talk to them about what you have learned in reading this book and how you hope it will reduce conflict and increase effective decision-making on behalf of your children. Make clear your commitment to change and then ask for help. Share this book with your coach. Ask that he or she takes time to read it carefully and be prepared to support you in this effort by coaching you.

If you are the person who has agreed to be a BIFF coach, either because you are a friend or family member or because you are a professional counselor or coach, this chapter will equip you to help others practice the BIFF process simply and effectively. Since Bill wrote the first edition of BIFF and staff at the High Conflict Institute began coaching for BIFF messages, thousands of people have benefited from being coached. The BIFF method has been used by business professionals, human resource professionals, neighbors, parents (both of adults and minors,) and by parents trying to work effectively with their coparents.

# The Approach to Coaching for a BIFF Message

The primary goal of coaching when it comes to using the BIFF approach is to help the coparent become more and more effective with the BIFF method. The coaching suggestions focus on equipping and encouraging that parent rather than showing how to do it or doing it for him or her.

As you have already read in this book, the purpose for using the BIFF method is to communicate in a way that does not cause defensiveness in the person on the receiving end. Responding with BIFF eliminates defensiveness, increases calmness and contains conflict.

Using the BIFF approach is about changing how a person communicates, which means it is specific to each person. There is no single *right* way to write a BIFF message. We have found that it is crucial to make this clear at the beginning of coaching.

Coaching for BIFF communications is targeted at strengthening the writer's use of the method, helping them learn to use it more and more effectively until it becomes habit for them. From the start, the coach should think of their role as a guide, leading the BIFF writer to remain in control of the communication. Effective coaching requires avoiding correcting the client. Rather, we have found it more helpful to ask questions that allows the BIFF writer to assess the effectiveness of his or her own work.

That being said, there is a place for coaches to offer observations at the very end of the coaching process. This placement is intentional. Remember, the long-term goal is for the client to develop such strong skills with the method that coaching is rarely needed. So, as you ask the first nine questions (listed below), be careful not to slip into making suggestions or critiques. Rather, ask each question and give the client the time to really think it through. If he or she turns the question back on you, we have found it much more effective if you use that as an opportunity to continue asking good questions that will help the writer look deeper into what he or she can see in his or her own work. This will continue to help strengthen his or her own knowledge of the method and have confidence in his or her own writing.

As a coach, the place to begin is by helping the client assess their own communication using these ten questions:

1. Is it Brief?
2. Is it Informative?
3. Is it Friendly?
4. Is it Firm?
5. Does it contain any Advice?
6. Does it contain any Admonishments?
7. Does it contain any Apologies?
8. How do you think the other person will respond?
9. Is there anything you would take out, add or change?
10. **Would you like to hear my thoughts about it?**

# Getting Started

It is not surprising that coparents often feel very vulnerable. They are passionate about the care of their children, want to do right by them, all while making decisions with someone displaying high conflict behavior. Some of that behavior may be things like criticizing them relentlessly, blaming them for anything available, and at times, attacking them through social media, in direct written communication or through their children. Too often the BIFF writer's response is to attack back in an attempt to return to a sense of stability themselves. This is a time when good coaching can really help; however, it is also a time when the writer can feel very vulnerable even to the coaching.

Creating a sense of safety within the coaching is crucial. As a coach, you want the BIFF writer to know, feel, and experience that you are supportive of the hard work they are doing. It can be helpful at first to remind the writer that the goal is to communicate about problem-solving without continuing an argument or creating defensiveness in the other parent. Also, you can remind him or her to stay focused on the problem being addressed and then begin asking the ten questions. As a coach, your response to their answers should remain positive and supportive.

You can introduce the 10 questions with an explanation like this:

> "Whenever we write a BIFF message, it helps to discuss it with someone before it is sent. When I've given my BIFF drafts to someone else, they have usually suggested that I trim them down—sometimes even cutting them in half! And I've usually agreed! It's hard to see in our own messages what might trigger more anger or defensiveness from the other person. It's often easier for someone else to spot trigger words or sentences. Let's start out by going through your BIFF message using a few questions. This will help you get better and better at writing BIFF messages that accomplish what you want.

First, I would like you to read your BIFF message out loud. Then, I'm going to ask you ten questions, so we can think about your BIFF message together. Remember, there's no exact right way to write a BIFF message. It depends on three things: 1) who is writing the BIFF message; 2) who is receiving it and, 3) what the situation is. And you are the person who knows these three things better than anyone. My goal is to help you think about whether the message as you have written it will accomplish what *you* want with the person *you* are dealing with."

# The BIFF Part of the Message

To get started, ask the first question. The client's answer is typically a short and to the point, "Yes." Resist the urge to engage in offering your own opinion at that time. Even if the client asks for your feedback right away, it is better to insist on waiting until you have been through all the questions. Remember the purpose is to help the client do his or her own analysis of the message, thereby facilitating a learning experience.

Each question does not demand an extensive discussion. Often clients will say things like, "Yes, I think it is informative." It is okay to simply roll on to the next question and ask, "And, do you think it is friendly?" At this point in the process you will go quickly or slowly based on the level of analysis done by the client.

## The Triple A's

The Triple A's are: Advice, Admonishments and Apologies, as explained in Chapter Three. If the BIFF writer is not familiar with the Triple A's or has forgotten them, you can briefly explain these when you ask questions 5-7:

5.  **"Does the BIFF message contain any Advice?** By this, I mean are you telling the other person how to deal with a particular problem a particular way? Unsolicited advice almost always triggers a defensive and often attacking response back at you. Unless the person you're dealing with *specifically* asked for your advice, it's almost always better not to give it—especially in a BIFF message that's intended to end the conversation or give two limited choices. So, do you see any advice in your BIFF as its currently written?"

6.  **"Does it contain any Admonishments?** In other words, are you speaking to the person like a parent telling a child how to behave? This never works in a BIFF message. When people are feeling defensive, the last thing they want is for you to tell them they are doing something wrong. The whole point of a BIFF message is to calm yourself down and end the conversation without triggering a defensive response. Do you see any hint of criticism in your BIFF as it is currently written?"

7.  **"Does it contain any Apologies?** This can be confusing. In general, apologies are a good thing. However, if you are dealing with a high-conflict person, he or she may tend to use your apologies against you, like ammunition. Avoid apologizing for anything of substance, like: "I shouldn't have done such-and-such." Or: "I'm sorry I hurt you by doing xyz." Or: "I guess my strategy failed." Or: "I know I haven't been sensitive to your needs." These types of apologies blame you and

Blamespeakers are preoccupied with blame, and will use it to prove that it really is All YOUR Fault! Of course, social apologies may be okay, like "I'm sorry to see that you're in this difficult situation." Or you could use the word "saddened" — "I'm saddened to see that you're in this difficult situation." With this in mind, do you see any apologies in what you have written?

## Your Thoughts

And now you are finally to question #10 (**Would you like to hear my thoughts about it?**) where you have opportunity to offer your thoughts, but only if the BIFF writer responds affirmatively. This is still not a time where it is most helpful to dazzle your client with your brilliant insight. Often you can share your thoughts by asking more detailed or direct questions. Remain in a place of learning and not knowing. If you think that the message is far too long, it is okay to ask some questions about what it would be like if some passages are left out or asking about if a particular sentence or three might bring up something that would cause defensiveness. If you have noticed that a pertinent piece of information has been left out, you can ask about the purpose in not including it. Sometimes it is effective to ask if you can read a part of the message back to the BIFF writer. This will often foster insight as they hear it from a different perspective, possibly even how the other parent may perceive it.

When the BIFF writer asks you for suggestions for change, you have a great opportunity to affirm their good work and their commitment to writing BIFF messages. You can say something like, "You are doing such a good job at putting this message together, why don't you write the changes first and let's see how it goes." Remember, your coachee is likely to be a bit shaky about all this. They are likely used to being criticized and told what to do by the other parent. You can offer a very different experience by finding as much good as possible in what they are doing.

If you decide that a suggestion is in order, either because your client had gotten stuck or just needs a little boost, it is good to come from their perspective. If you offer a couple of choices the writer will be able to engage in making the words their own. Try something like, "What it seems like you are trying to communicate is ... or maybe it is something a little more like, ... Do either of those work for you? How would you need to change that to make it work?" Keep emphasizing the good work the writer is doing. Your goal is to show support and encouragement that he or she is capable and doing well. Keeping the writer responsible for writing the content is empowering for him or her and a good indication that BIFFs may have a chance to become the norm in future.

Often, just the act of reading the message out loud reveals changes that need to be made. Once the writer hears the content and decides to make the change, be sure to affirm them. When it is rewritten, ask to hear it again, and again. Ask what the BIFF writer thinks of it each time. Don't jump to just affirm it. Remember, it's up to them—not you. More than anything else, you are helping the writer learn to engage a process of self-analysis. In a sense you are helping the writer learn to have an inner voice that is reflective and supportive.

# A Stepparent Example

Suppose your coachee, Kalani, has written this message to her ex-husband, Kaleb, regarding his new girlfriend, Valentina:

> **Kalani to Kaleb**: It's come to my attention that Valentina has taken our daughter shopping for a bathing suit three months before summer. You know that this is something I always like to do with our daughter, especially now that she's starting puberty. It feels like Valentina is trying to jump the gun and create a special relationship with our daughter that's inappropriate since you've only known her for a month. I am concerned that you are trying to have Valentina replace me in our daughter's eyes. She has even told me that you are going to ask for more parenting time so you can be a "happy little family." What are you up to?

As Kalani's coach, ask her all nine questions to get her thinking as she reflects on this email. Suppose she likes it as is. Then, after asking her question #10, she agrees to have you tell her your thoughts about it. It could go like this:

**Coach**: "Overall, I like it. However, I'm concerned that the last three sentences may escalate things unnecessarily. Are they necessary? And is there another, better way to say what you are aiming for here?"

**Kalani**: "Well, I want to tell her to cut it out. I don't like what she's doing. She seems to want to replace me in our daughter's eyes and I'm afraid she will convince Kaleb to go along with her. She's very aggressive."

**Coach**: "Well, it's up to you, of course. But from what

you've told me, I don't think you will get her to change just with an email. I would suggest perhaps setting up a meeting to define what is appropriate and what's not. Since its early in Kaleb's relationship with her, you might head off some problems before they really start. After all, this is a gray area for most people after a separation or divorce. It might be better to have a meeting that focuses on boundaries, rather than intent. If you express that she has ill-intent, it may make things worse unnecessarily. Or you could just suggest some boundaries in an email."

**Kalani**: "I'll have to think about it."

**Coach**: "Why don't you try writing something that focuses on who does what, rather than addressing his or her intentions."

**Kalani**: "Ok, I'll try that.

---

**Kalani to Kaleb**: It's come to my attention that Valentina has taken our daughter shopping for a bathing suit three months before summer. You know that this is something I always like to do with our daughter, especially now that she's starting puberty. I would suggest that you tell Valentina to slow down and let me buy the more intimate apparel for our daughter at this time in her development. Thanks for respecting these types of mother-daughter issues. And if Valentina wants to discuss any of this, please tell her to feel free to call me.

---

**Coach**: "Sounds much more positive! Do you like it? I like how you focused on the specific issue rather than making it bigger. And even if they do want to have a 'happy little family,' this lets them know that you are being assertive about them respecting your role."

**Kalani**: "Thanks! I think you're right. This sounds a lot better."

**Coach**: "Great! Let me know how it works out after you send it."

And then you can tell yourself (privately): "Way to go, Coach!"

## A Home Repair Example

Suppose your client is Jade who recently moved out of the family residence; however, both parents still own the home and he has always done the home maintenance. He received this email from his soon-to-be ex-wife, Jill:

**Jill to Jade**: Hi Jade—you are totally irresponsible! You didn't take care of that leak with the irrigation system in the back yard. Now the water bill says we owe a lot more. Something's really wrong out there and it's all your fault! You better get to work back there and don't blame me just because I don't want you in the house while you deal with it.

Jade calls you to be his BIFF coach. You might start out with the following:

"First of all, if you feel attacked and defensive, you are having a normal human response. However, it will make your life easier if you don't respond defensively. Instead, tell yourself that personal attacks are about the attacker, not about you. Then, try writing a BIFF response. Let me explain how that works, then you can draft a BIFF response and we can discuss it."

Then, Jade sends you the following draft BIFF response and you set up a meeting to discuss it. Here's his first try:

> **Jade to Jill**: Dear Jill.... thank you for reminding me about the leak in the back yard. I'll check it out this weekend. We may have to hire someone to fix it because I think it's beyond my skills. And I don't appreciate your insults. They won't get the job done any faster. Sincerely—Jade

Suppose you go through the first 7 questions and he decides that his message is Brief, Informative, Friendly and Firm, and he doesn't see any Advice, Admonishments or Apologies. You tell him he's done an amazing job for his first attempt at a BIFF response. Then, you can continue with the remaining questions:

**8. How do you think the other person will respond?**

**Jade**: "With the information I've given her, I think she should calm down. Although she may not like my comment about her insult, she will find a way to defend it."

**9. Then, is there anything you would take out, add or change to deal with that?**

**Jade**: "I'm wondering whether I should take out these sentences: 'And I don't appreciate your insults. They won't get the job done any faster.'"

**Coach**: "Try reading it out loud with the sentences, and then read it out loud without them and see which one sounds better to you."

Jade reads it both ways out loud. Then, he says: "It's definitely better without those sentences. She's more likely to be positive about this situation without them. What do you think?"

**Coach**: "It also sounded better to me without those sentences. But you know her better than I do and it's your BIFF. So, it's up to you."

**10. Would you like to hear my thoughts about it?**

**Jade**: "Yes. Definitely."

At this point you, as his coach, can make any suggestions, so don't hold back important ideas. But also don't overwhelm him with too many thoughts about it. Remember to be encouraging. And it may be that you don't have any additional thoughts because he caught the one issue that you also recognized. This is often what happens if you just ask the client the nine questions before you give your feedback, if there's anything left to suggest by then.

## Conclusion

By now you have probably figured out, coaching for BIFF messages is about equipping your BIFF writers to no longer need your services. Using the 10 BIFF Coaching Questions will help you keep the focus on the BIFF writer and their self-analysis. It helps the writer remember what he or she is trying to accomplish with the message, and to make all the editing decisions. Over time, BIFF writers can learn to take the time to go through the questions and make the edits even when you are not available. Encourage the writer to have someone review messages before sending them, and talk through how the writer has answered the questions for himself or herself. The more this is done, the better he or she will be at writing BIFF messages right from the start.

The 10 BIFF Coaching Questions help you, the coach, remember your role and hold back the urge to *tell* rather than *ask*. Remember, you will be much more effective if you affirm the BIFF writer's abilities, support their development, and leave them feeling competent and able. This is not the time to draw attention to yourself; rather, it is an opportunity to encourage more peaceful communication to promote a growth mindset in that person.

# CHAPTER TWELVE

# You Decide

You are in charge of your behavior and you decide how you will live out of your values. The ways that you interact with your coparent are your responsibility and yours alone. The intention that you bring to these encounters is crucial. If you intend to be a successful problem-solver and a cooperative coparent you will likely be helped by paying attention to your own skills and abilities and carefully developing them instead of focusing on your coparent's deficits. This final chapter is about where to focus your attention to get the best results.

Early in this book we talked about two fundamental differences in how our brains deal with conflict. On one hand we are better at problem-solving when we feel safe. On the other hand, when we feel threatened, we switch to fast, defensive reacting to protect ourselves from real and perceived dangers.

Regardless of where in the brain these responses are controlled, we have some choice in how we respond and others respond to us. When someone comes charging at you verbally (hopefully not physically), our defensive reactions are triggered in our brains. Yet we have within us the ability to override certain brain reactions with more effective responses as we grow and learn but it takes practice.

What we have learned from BIFF communications is that when we use positive useful written information, we get a similar response instead of a continuation of the angry or misinformed communication that we were sent. It is rewarding to hear that some upset people are responding to BIFF responses in a similar format (even when they don't even know the format).

Likewise, when we put out negative useless venting or counter-attacks, we tend to get emotional useless venting and attacking in return. In other words, we get to decide how other people will respond to us. If we can develop skills at managing our own emotions and responses, we will be able to influence (but not control) the responses of others.

## Managing Your Own Danger Signals

We find that being aware of our inner messages is crucial to successfully managing interactions with people who tend toward high conflict behaviors. It will be no surprise that you will do a better job of responding if you are well-rested, physically active on a regular basis, and eating a healthful diet. The more stress, the more important it is that we take good care of ourselves. And beyond just taking care of yourself, you will need to practice paying attention to yourself.

Too often feelings get a bad reputation particularly when difficult behavior can so easily be blamed on having had certain feelings. It is important to have a basic understanding of what feelings are for, so that they can be allowed to function as they are meant to. It might be helpful to think of feelings like the indicator lights on a dashboard. They are there to draw your attention to something else. They are not meant to be paid attention to themselves. When you get hungry, the problem is not the hunger itself—the problem is lack of nutrition. When you get something to eat, the hunger goes away. Emotional feelings behave in the same way. They come up to draw our attention to something other than themselves. When we follow their lead and pay attention, the feeling will most likely go away.

The practice of mindfulness is an effective way to train our left brain to listen to our right brain. Mindfulness lets you learn to practice being respectful of your feelings without being distracted by them. They *come on* to carry a message, but not to be the message themselves. By taking the time to sit and *listen* to what our emotions are trying to tell us, we learn to hear ourselves. And in doing so, we learn to know when we are irritated before we get frustrated, and know that we are frustrated before we are mad, and know when we are mad before we get furious. A person does not manage oneself well once a feeling has progressed to the maximum experience of it, whether it is pain, fury, starvation or ecstasy. We manage ourselves much more effectively at the level of irritation, frustration, and enjoyment. And so, learning to pay attention to ourselves and our own feedback systems allows us to manage ourselves so much more effectively.

There are many different ways to enter into the practice of mindfulness. Some, like yoga, involve the entire body, mind, and emotions at the same time. Others use music, or writing, or other art forms to direct the mind and emotions. Finding one that fits for you and practicing it regularly will help you have deeper resources for engaging in coparenting with someone who readily exhibits high conflict behaviors.

Most of us can overcome an initial upset. We experience our own emotions, settle ourselves quickly and move on. For example, someone says something negative about us. While we do experience the sense of separation that can come with criticism, or the pain of rejection, we can settle ourselves quickly. Blamespeakers start from a place of heightened defensiveness, escalate quickly and stay stuck in that place. They are then not able to engage in meaningful problem-solving, because strong defensiveness tends to shut down logical problem-solving.

But just because a person tends toward escalated drama does not mean that all is lost. In fact, the entire premise of BIFF is that it is possible to invite people into a different mindset, that it is possible to nudge them into a different *frame of mind*. Most of the time, by making the choice to use good BIFF responses, you can focus their attention away from their upset emotions (right brain defensiveness) and onto problem-solving. With practice, persistence, and a fair amount of compassion, it appears that you may be able to shift a person's attention away from their own unmanageable emotions and actions and onto more reasonable thinking and behaving. Don't get distracted by the drama. Don't let the other person define the conversation. Quickly move to conversation that is Brief, Informative, Friendly, and Firm.

**Brief**: By keeping it brief, there is less potentially negative information to trigger defensiveness. Almost anyone can tolerate a little negative information, or a small upset. But, as the challenging piece is left there too long, without relief, it becomes more and more difficult to stay away from the sense of being threatened that triggers the right brain defensiveness.

**Informative**: This seems to direct their minds to the analytical, left brain problem-solving approach. That's why it's so important to keep this information strictly neutral, rather than judgmental, negative or disrespectful.

**Friendly**: Maintaining a friendly tone, an open posture, and an upbeat attitude can often help another person back out of a defensive and fearful place. People who feel threatened quickly move to all-or-nothing thinking and behaving. A good sense of humor can disarm the situation and return a sense of calm. It is challenging to do this without appearing to be patronizing. Still, when you can be informative and friendly, at the same time, the combination often helps others slide back out of right-brain defensiveness and into thoughtful problem solving.

**Firm**: Clear boundaries are often comforting, even if they are sometimes constraining. Refusing to engage in an argument is a boundary. And when the other person is shown respect in a calm, focused, neutral way, often they can let go of the conflict and get to a calm place again. Staying focused on the problem that is to be solved, rather than chasing off after a distraction will also help reduce a person's defensiveness.

# Turning Off Blamespeak in Your Life

We live in a culture where complaining is often substituted for problem-solving, where blaming is the replacement for responsibility, and where arguing is confused with healthy conflict. If you are going to foster an atmosphere of cooperation and effective coparenting, it will be important to manage your environment, and what you use to influence your thinking.

Start with a commitment to personal responsibility and avoiding Blamespeak. When we see ourselves as victims, we are more likely to be defensive. When we begin from a sense of defensiveness, we are more likely to react quickly with high conflict behavior, escalating the situation.

Build your accountability team with people who encourage you to live up to your own values, and to grow toward more personal responsibility, and less blamespeak. Protect your thinking by limiting what you listen to, watch and read. Our culture has become dramatically more hostile over the last generation. It is far too easy to take on the attitudes of those around who are negative and often hostile. Find sources of support for the direction you want to go, and the person you want to be, and use them as constant reinforcement.

We are more and more aware of the danger of infectious diseases. Blamespeak can act like an infectious agent. It can quickly take hold and spread from person to person. Now, we are not suggesting that you in any way avoid reality. And coparenting with a person who is prone to high conflict behavior can be quite challenging. Be honest with yourself about what you are experiencing but surround yourself with people who are positive, who believe in your ability to manage yourself effectively, and who will encourage you to be kind, and gracious. Work hard to make decisions from a place of facts and real information. You will feel better about yourself, your parenting, and your work with your coparent. All of that will lead to a better life for your children.

# APPENDICES

# Top 12 Tips for CoParent Boundaries*

By Bill Eddy, LCSW, Esq.

When parents separate, their lives need more clearly defined boundaries for their sake and for the children. Two of the most important parenting skills are managing one's own stress and modeling healthy adult relationship communication. Setting boundaries individually and jointly can protect children from situations when they might be exposed to too much of their parent's distress and also show them that their separated parents can successfully manage their new lives.

The following 12 tips can help:

1. **It's About the Children**

   It's easy to get wrapped up in setting, defending or pushing boundaries because of issues between the parents. After all, everything is different after parents separate and the need for boundaries is much stronger. However, the focus should always be on the children and what's in their best interest. Sometimes stronger boundaries are worth fighting for (for the children's benefit) and other times it's best to be flexible (for the children's benefit).

Ask yourself which would be less stressful for the children in the long run. If you're unsure, get consultation or advice. With rare exceptions, they are expected to have a significant relationship with both parents. So, don't give the appearance of trying to block your child's relationship with the other parent, while still having reasonable boundaries to avoid exposing them to too much stress.

2. **Separate Homes—Really**

As soon as possible, it's best to have respect for each other's privacy by establishing rights and rules about the family residence. The easiest way to think about rules is to think of the parent who stays (if that's possible) as the *tenant* and the two of you as the *landlord*. Don't come over except by the agreement of the tenant. Don't make big decisions without the agreement of the other landlord (like selling the home or breaking a lease).

The former family residence is now one coparent's residence, just as the other coparent's new residence is treated as his/her separate space. Sometimes parents agree to change the locks. Of course, if there are restraining orders, access may be restricted by court order and the orders should be strictly followed.

3. **Parenting Time—and Place**

In the early stages of most separations, it's best to establish clearly separate time with the children, without the other parent present. Some parents continue to live together for a while or the *out-parent* has their parenting time at the family residence. This arrangement can work in some cases, but it should be very short-term, so that the *out-parent* does not feel limited or judged while caring for the children, and the *in-parent* does not feel crowded and unable to have privacy. Some parents attempt to be *gatekeepers* between the child and the other parent, but this is not standard and should only occur when court orders say so.

4. **Parenting Decisions**
   Each parent should have sole decision-making authority in his or her home regarding rules and responsibilities, bedtimes and chores, during his or her parenting time. Each should be allowed to make occasional suggestions to the other, but they are only suggestions. It's up to the *on-duty* parent to decide if they want to use the suggestions. There may be some good ideas to consider, so be open-minded. But children also need to learn that there is more than one way of doing things. If there's on-going dispute about major joint parenting decisions or the overall parenting schedule, they should be made with professional assistance, such as with a mediator or other professional.

5. **Picking Up the Children**
   Exchanges between coparents can be one of the most stressful times for children. There is a range of levels of boundaries that parents can set.

   First is simply agreeing not to discuss *issues* in front of the children during an exchange. While it may seem convenient, it can easily escalate into conflict.

Second is not being around each other during an exchange, such as having one parent pick up the children by staying in the car at the curbside in front of the home.

Third is not being at the same location at all, such as having each parent pick up the children at school and return to school.

Fourth is having exchanges supervised by a neutral third person, such as a relative or friend, or even a professional if necessary.

Fifth is neither parent should videotape, record or bring hostile associates to a parenting exchange.

Sixth is avoid calling the police if there is a difficult exchange. Protect the children from such a humiliating experience and discuss it later away from the children, such as with a lawyer or counselor or mediator.

## 6. Contact During Other Parent's Time

When coparents have good communication, they still respect each other's time with the children. So, phone calls should be at reasonable times from the other parent and from the child. When communication is potentially tense, then setting a schedule for phone calls can help, such as Tuesday and Thursday evening between 7:00 – 7:30pm. If communication is disruptive or very difficult, it may be best to have no calls in or out of the other parent's home. Children often feel relieved that they do not have to talk to one parent while at the other's home.

It reduces the likelihood that they will be quizzed by one or both parents about their activities or the call.

7. **Children's Events**

Special events for the children, such as sports or school events, should be about the children. If the parents can tolerate being at the same event—and the child wants you both there—then make every effort to make it a positive experience without raising any *issues*. If it could be tense, then plan to have no interaction and sit in separate areas. If it could be extremely tense, then parents should take turns attending these special occasions, or strictly follow the parenting schedule so that the parent caring for the child only attends events that occur during their time.

8. **Contact between the CoParents**

If there is ongoing tension between the parents, many agree to simply communicate by email except in emergencies. Court orders in high-conflict cases often require that the parents communicate only by email. Many courts order parents to communicate via coparenting communication apps that keep track of communications so that parents are more respectful and issues of parent communication can be reviewed if necessary later on.

9. **Writing Emails and Texts**

One method of writing emails is the BIFF Response® method, which was especially designed for responding to hostility in writing. This method involves making emails Brief, Informative, Friendly and Firm. *Brief* usually means just a paragraph or two, so the email doesn't say more than absolutely necessary. *Informative* means no opinions, emotions, defenses, advice or admonishments—just straight information, such as Who will do What, When and Where. *Friendly* means including a friendly greeting (Thanks for responding...) or closing. *Firm* doesn't mean harsh—it means ending the conversation without one last challenge to the other person or starting a new conflict.

## 10. Avoid Using Children as Messengers

One of the most common mistakes separated parents make is to tell the children to tell the other parent some piece of information. It may seem very convenient, since we do this all the time with adults. But it can be very stressful for the child, who is rightfully afraid he or she will suffer the other parent's anger or irritation with the message. If important information is needed, then the parent should use email. If its urgent, a text message could be sufficient.

## 11. Discussions Away from the Children

If there are likely difficult phone calls or in-person conversations between the coparents, they should be held away from the children. This means closing the door to a room where the conversation or phone call takes place. This also means being careful not to make disparaging remarks about the other parent in the presence of the child nor allowing others to do so. (This is a common court order.) In the event that a disparaging remark is made (no one is perfect), it is important to make a *repairing comment* that lets the child know that you really do support the other parent's relationship with the child and don't mean to disrespect that.

## 12. Discussions with the Children

Each parent should be able to discuss anything with the children without restriction by the other parent. But each parent should also use wisdom in having appropriate boundaries on what topics they discuss with the child. Parents should avoid quizzing the child about the other parent's household or social life. On the other hand, it's normal and appropriate to ask a child in general terms "How are you doing? How was your weekend?" That's part of learning social skills. If the child wants to talk about their time at the other parent's home, that should be fine. If not, that should be fine too.

If one parent is concerned that the other parent is being unsafe or abusive, that parent should avoid quizzing the child and instead consult with a professional about what to do. Children who are repeatedly questioned become less reliable sources of information and more stressed. Better to keep such concerns out of your own relationship with the children, so that they can focus on being children and being happy when they are with you.

*This article first appeared in the March 2016 issue of the monthly eNews of the international organization Association of Family and Conciliation Courts (AFCC).*

# What to Tell the Children About a High Conflict CoParent

By Bill Eddy, LCSW, Esq.

*Many parents have asked us about how to raise a child or children with a coparent (whether a spouse, former spouse or unmarried partner) who is high conflict. In other words, the coparent frequently exhibits some or all of the following:*

- **Preoccupied with blaming others** (often those closest to him/her, like the child or the other parent—or both)

- **All-or-nothing thinking** (solutions to problems have to be all their way; they see some people (including themselves) as all-good and others (including you) as all-bad; may see one of his or her children as all-good and the other as all-bad)

- **Unmanaged emotions** (screaming, crying, pleading—but some don't show this).

- **Extreme behaviors** (like yelling, hitting spouse or child, making false allegations, spreading rumors, hiding money, and so forth)

*If you are a parent who is asking this question, it is very important to avoid being accused of "bad-mouthing" the other parent, by speaking negatively about him or her to the children and providing too much information about adult issues, such as a court case. On the other hand, you want to protect your children from the blaming and uncontrolled behavior of the high-conflict coparent, and to provide the children with coping skills and help them not blame themselves.*

*This article discusses one way parents can deal with both concerns, while helping your children to be resilient throughout their lives.*

# Teach 4 Big Skills™

Rather than talking to the kids about the *high conflict* coparent (and you should never use that term around the children), talk about the 4 Big Skills™ for life. These skills are:

1. Flexible thinking
2. Managed emotions
3. Moderate behaviors
4. Checking ourselves to see if we're using these skills (and not blaming others)

Tell your children that these are 4 Big Skills that will help them with friends, help them get a good job someday, and may help them be community leaders someday, if they want. These 4 Big Skills help in any relationship, whether it's someone you like or someone you don't like. You can explain this to a child of almost any age, starting at least at age four, if you put it in simple terms.

Then, in daily life you can ask them if they noticed other people who used these skills in solving problems, or if you used any of these 4 Big Skills in solving a problem. For example:

- "Did you notice how that guy at the store was frustrated, but he stayed calm and listened to the clerk tell him where to find what he wanted? Would you say he was managing his emotions?"

- "Did you notice how that guy on TV was just yelling at a store clerk. Would you say he was managing his emotions? Did he seem to get what he wanted? No, he didn't. How do you think he could have used managed emotions to help solve his problem?"

An example you could share about yourself: "Today I was really frustrated by sitting still in a traffic jam. But I told myself to think about things I was looking forward to this week—like your birthday party, and seeing my sister, and a movie I want to see someday. I used my flexible thinking and managed my emotions. But it wasn't easy. I kept having bad thoughts about the other drivers in front of me, but then I chose my happy thoughts again. Did you have any frustrating times today that you dealt with by using your flexible thinking?"

## Help Your Child Cope with Friends

Once you've started to have these casual discussions with your child, you can teach these skills when they have a conflict with a friend. For example: "Mom/Dad, this kid at school says he hates me! I feel like punching him in the nose! He/she used to be my best friend!"

Then, you could say something like: "Oh, that's too bad. I remember when that happened to me. I can understand how angry you must have felt. But I'm glad you didn't punch him/her in the nose. Have you thought of what you can do instead? Maybe you can talk with him/her, after you've both calmed down. Try to use your flexible thinking to come up with ideas of what went wrong and how you can solve it."

You can also do this when conflicts come up between siblings, and especially praise them when they solve their own problems. You could say: "I'm really glad that you both were able to solve this problem on your own. You're pretty good problem-solvers, especially when you use your flexible thinking like you just did." Catch them when they're doing well. (You get more of what you pay attention to.)

## Help Your Child Cope with Your CoParent

Now, since you have taken an educational approach to teaching the 4 Big Skills, you can start using them when things happen with your coparent. Suppose he or she was unreasonably angry at your child, and the child came to you to complain. Rather than saying that your coparent is a jerk, you could say: "Remember, some people have a harder time managing their emotions than other people. When you're ready, let's do some flexible thinking about ways you might deal with situations like that in the future. In the meantime, we can manage our own emotions, even though some other people can't."

By speaking in this *teaching skills* way about the other parent, you avoid *bad-mouthing* him or her, while giving your child skills for resilience—for a lifetime. This way, you can't be blamed for saying anything specifically about your coparent. Instead, you have kept it as a general lesson and still provided a discussion about what to do in the future in *situations like that.*

By teaching the 4 Big Skills for life, your child can learn lessons that will last into adulthood, even during the most difficult times of childhood—including separation and divorce.

# Calming Upset People with EAR*

By Bill Eddy, LCSW, Esq.

Everyone gets upset some of the time. High conflict people get upset a lot of the time. A simple technique called an EAR Statement® can help you calm others down. This is especially helpful if you are in a close relationship, such as dealing with a coparent after a separation or divorce. High conflict people tend to emotionally attack those closest to them when they are frustrated and can't manage their own emotions. The intensity of their uncontrolled emotions can really catch you off-guard. But if you practice making EAR Statements you can really connect with upset people, which is really what they want.

## EAR Statements

EAR stands for Empathy, Attention and Respect. It is the opposite of what you feel like giving someone when he or she is upset and verbally attacking YOU! Yet you will be amazed at how effective this is when you do it right. It really is rather simple, but it takes practice, practice, practice.

An EAR Statement connects with the person's experience, with their feelings. For example, let's say that someone verbally attacks you for not replying to a text message as quickly as he or she would have liked. "You don't respect me! You don't care how long I have to wait to deal with this problem! You're not a responsible parent!"

Rather than defending yourself, give the person an EAR Statement, such as: "Wow, I can hear how upset you are. Tell me what's going on. I share your concerns about this problem and respect your efforts to solve it." This statement included:

EMPATHY:    "I can hear how upset you are."

ATTENTION:  "Tell me what's going on."

RESPECT:    "I respect your efforts."

## The Importance of Empathy

Empathy is different from sympathy. Having empathy for someone means that you can feel the pain and frustration that they are feeling, and probably have felt similar feelings in your own life. These are normal human emotions and they are normally triggered in the people nearby. (Emotions are contagious!) When you show empathy for another person, you are treating them as a peer who you are concerned about and can relate to as an equal in distress.

Sympathy is when you see someone else in a bad situation that you are not in. You may feel sorry for them and have sympathy for them, but it is a one-up and one-down position. There is more of a separation between those who give sympathy and those who receive it.

You don't have to use the word *empathy* to make a statement that shows empathy. For example:

"I can see how important this is to you."

"I understand this can be frustrating."

"I know this process can be confusing."

"I'm saddened to see that you're in this situation."

"I'd like to help you if I can."

"Let's see if we can solve this together."

## The Importance of Attention

There are many ways to let a person know that you will pay attention. For example, you can say:

"I will listen as carefully as I can."

"I will pay attention to your concerns."

"Tell me what's going on."

"Tell me more!"

You can also show attention non-verbally, such as:

- Have good "eye contact" (keeping your eyes focused on the person)

- Nod your head up and down to show that you are attentive to their concerns

- Lean in to pay closer attention

- Put your hand near them, such as on the table beside them (but be careful about touching an upset HCP – it may be misinterpreted as a threat, a come-on, or a put-down)

## The Importance of Respect

Anyone in distress, and especially HCPs, need respect from others. Even the most difficult and upset person usually has some quality that you can respect. By recognizing that quality, you can calm a person who is desperate to be respected. Here are several statements showing respect:

"I can see that you are a hard worker."
"I respect your commitment to solving this problem."
"I respect your efforts on this."
"I respect your success at accomplishing _____."
"You have important skills that we need here."

## Why EAR is so Important to HCPs

They're not getting it anywhere else. They have usually alienated most of the people around them. It is the last thing that anyone wants to give them. They are used to being rejected, abandoned, insulted, ignored, and disrespected by those around them. They are starving for empathy, attention and respect. They are looking for it anywhere they can get it. So just give it to them. It's free and you don't sacrifice anything. You can still set limits, give bad news, and keep a social or professional distance. It just means that you can connect with them around solving a particular problem and treat them like an equal human being, whether you agree or strongly disagree with their part in the problem.

## What to Avoid

- Don't Lie.
- You don't have to listen forever.
- EAR doesn't mean you agree.
- Maintain an "arms-length" relationship.

## Manage Your Amygdala

Of course, this is the opposite of what we feel like doing. You may think to yourself: "No way I'm going to listen to this after how I've been verbally attacked!" But that's just your amygdala talking, in an effort to protect you from danger. Our brains are very sensitive to threats, especially your amygdala (you actually have two, one in the middle of your right hemisphere and one in the middle of your left). Most people, while growing up, learn to manage the impulsive, protective responses of their amygdala and override them with a rational analysis of the situation, using their prefrontal context behind the forehead.

In fact, that is a lot of what adolescence is about: learning what is a crisis needing an instant, protective response (amygdala) and learning what situations are not a crisis and instead need a calm and rational response (prefrontal cortex). High conflict people often were abused or entitled growing up, and didn't have the secure, balanced connection necessary to learn these skills of emotional self-management. Therefore, you can help them by helping yourself not overreact to them—use your own prefrontal cortex to manage your amygdala.

## It's Not About You!

Remind yourself it's not about you! Don't take it personally. It's about the person's own upset and lack of sufficient skills to manage his or her own emotions. Try making EAR statements and you will find they often end the attack and calm the person down. This is especially true for high conflict people (HCPs) who regularly have a hard time calming themselves down.

All of these are calming statements. They let the person know that you want to connect with him or her, rather than threaten him or her.

## Conclusion

Making EAR statements—or non-verbally showing your Empathy, Attention and Respect—may help you avoid many potentially high-conflict situations. It can save you time, money and emotional energy for years to come.

*Note: A book called *Calming Upset People with EAR,* written by Bill Eddy, co-author of this book, and published by Unhooked Books, will contain about twenty examples of EAR Statements similar in the manner that this book on BIFF communications is structured.

## List of BIFF Examples

## Online Course for BIFF Practice

You can learn more about BIFF Responses and practice them in your own CoParenting Playbook at ConflictPlaybook. com: www.conflictplaybook.com/coparenting-playbook

# ACKNOWLEDGEMENTS

*Bill:* I would like to acknowledge my wife, Alice, who is my favorite BIFF coach. I thank Megan Hunter, co-founder and CEO of High Conflict Institute for nudging me forward in writing this book and several others, and finding a way to make them successful. I thank Annette Burns and Kevin Chafin for making this a smooth and easy co-writing project. And I want to acknowledge all of my clients who have helped me strengthen my skills and learn from their experience that BIFF communications really can work.

*Annette:* I would like to acknowledge the parents I've worked with over the years as either attorney or parenting coordinator and all they have taught me about communication and coparenting. For every poorly thought-out communication between coparents, I've experienced many, many solid, caring communications that restored my faith in coparenting.

*Kevin:* I would like to express thanks to the many who have guided and developed my thinking about families, therapy, and resolving conflict. Thank you to Donnie, Samuel and Lee Morehouse for the years of support and on the ground training. Thank you to Jill Katz for more than three decades of encouragement and comradery. Thank you to Simone Haberstock, the rest of the Missouri Chapter of the AFCC, and those who practice in the fields of Family Law and court involved therapy for the years of dialogue, discourse, consternation and collaboration. Thank you to Bill Eddy and Megan Hunter for the opportunity to participate in the development of this addition to the BIFF series, and to Annette Burns for just the right word at just the right time.

# THE AUTHORS

**BILL EDDY, LCSW, ESQ,** is the author of twenty + books, a lawyer, therapist, mediator and the co-founder and the Chief Innovation Officer of the High Conflict Institute. He developed the "High Conflict Personality" theory (HCP Theory) and has become an international expert on managing disputes involving high conflict personalities and personality disorders. He developed the New Ways for Families, New Ways for Work and New Ways for Mediation methods for handling divorce, workplace and mediation disputes and his *Psychology Today* blog has over 4 million views. His websites are: highconflictinstitute.com and conflictplaybook.com.

**ANNETTE T. BURNS, JD,** is an attorney and a certified Family Law Specialist, practicing in Arizona. She is a past president of the Association of Family and Conciliation Courts and is a Fellow of the American Academy of Matrimonial Lawyers. She has served on every Arizona Supreme Court Committee that created, adopted and revised the Arizona Rules of Family Law Procedure since 2003. She has received many awards for service to community, the practice of law, and to children. Her website is: heyannette.com

**KEVIN CHAFIN, LPC,** is a mediator and Licensed Professional Counselor in private practice in Kansas City, Missouri. He is the current president of the board of the Missouri Chapter of the Association of Family and Conciliation Courts. He has more than 30 years' experience with family and domestic court systems. Coparenting counseling is a large part of his practice, often with high conflict families. He is a regular presenter on topics related to mediation as well as court-involved counseling with parents and children. His website is: kevinchafinlpc.com